Magick Where You're At

By Giana Cicchelli

W&T Press
Ontario, California

First Edition
First Printing, 2016

Cover Design © 2016 by Giana Cicchelli
Cover Art © 2016 by Giana Cicchelli

ISBN 978-0985026653

Published by W&T Press, Imprint of Giana Cicchelli Publishing, Ontario, CA.

Printed in the United States of America

it
was
always
for you

I am not saying anything new about magick. I am showing you the way I understand it. We are portals for each other, and the way I explain the world of magick may be the secret key that unlocks the doorway of understanding for you. It may not. Always be in search of doorways that open and transport you further into understanding yourself and the world.

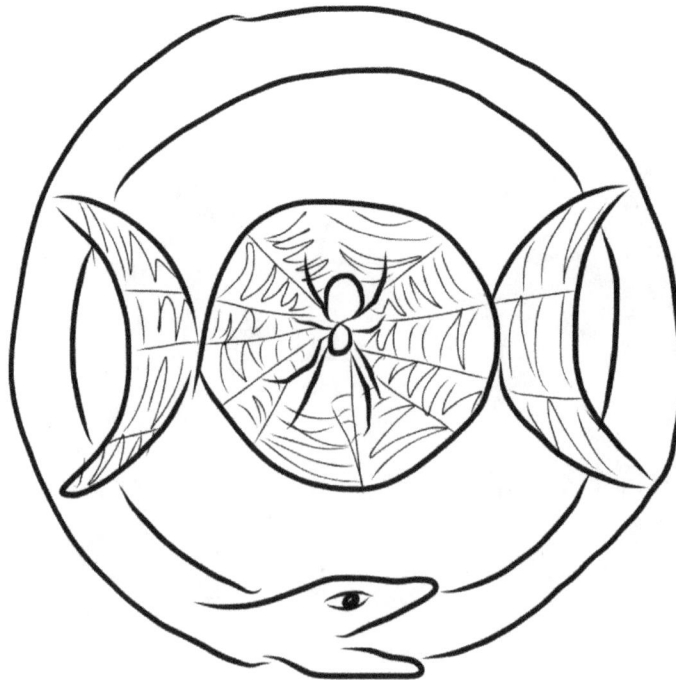

Contents

Preface

This is not an academic book. I can do academia, but this is not that. I often mention sociological connections in this book, because I know sociology. It is how I understand the world. I also find that sociology asks you to step outside of yourself, and question everything you have been taught, everything you thought was real. This is also true in magick, and in living the magickal lifestyle.

This is not an academic book, but rather a book that asks you to go *experience* magick for yourself. You can philosophize about magick all you want, but I'm asking you to experience it. Open yourself up to the great mysteries of the universe, and leap into that enchanting unknown. Full participation is required to engage in magick, and if you want to embark on this journey, you must allow yourself to suspend disbelief.

I wrote this book as a guide to help get you there, to the magick. I promise you it is much more all-inclusive than you suspect, and it will take you on the adventure of a lifetime (if not many lifetimes!). It will most assuredly not be easy, and sometimes it will be devastatingly hard, but with a heart full of faith in the existence of magick, in the existence of the ineffable, you will be rewarded with such profound mind-shattering revelations, that you could not imagine ever relinquishing this path. Know that the truth will change faces, and that nothing is static, it is all alive with magick. Your participation will grant you greater understanding of the interconnectedness of all.

1

It Starts Here

We are all looking for magick. We go to workshops, we search for teachers, we put our power and energy into the 'other' that their stories and guidance may bring us to our own magick. We hear stories of magick, and compare them to what we think is lacking in ours. Everyone owns magick, magick is life. Magick is the trees, and the birds, and the cosmos. We all have connection. When we look outside of ourselves for magick we are taken in by the ego of others, and then we build up their experiences as greater than our own. They are not. We are one, a mass of beings on a planet struggling to find a balance within ourselves, and with each other. In this struggle we hope for magick, and strive for it, as if it may or may not be real. Magick is real, and each one of us has access. Magick is real, and each one of us has experienced it. Those who haven't aren't paying attention. Magick is in every moment. Magick is life.

In this book I will introduce you to how I work with magick, or live the magickal lifestyle. It is a culmination of what I've learned, and how I've interpreted those learnings, with some practical applications, and stories to guide the way. If you don't like what I've said, then don't take it. It is not my desire to push dogma on to you, or to force you to live the way that I do. If you are reading this, however, chances are that you would like to learn a bit about how to live a magickal life. I believe I am presenting keys that will unlock it for you.

Know that every magickal experience I've had was not as amazing in the moment, as it was in the memory of that moment. This means that magick happens quite inconsequentially, and then in the retelling of the moment it becomes bigger, and bigger, and more colorful. This is what I've found from many magickal practitioners. This doesn't mean that magick is something small, but at the same time, it is very small. It gains revelatory dimensions when one looks back over it, and sees the interconnectedness of all of life. This is indeed a great magick. The moments of realizing you are not alone. We are all one, and we are all connected with the infinite.

In the moment, however, magick can be as simple as a spider riding on a leaf in the pool. As seemingly innocent as a raven cawing during a conversation. It is in the listening and paying attention that one begins to interact with the infinite. This interaction is magick. Magick grows with time, and with faith. At first you do not believe, as life has trained you that rationality has no place for magick. I disagree, I think magick is completely rational and logical. Magick does follow strict rules of accordance, but with attributes that are currently not able to be measured by western science. Once you realize that things unseen are still palpable then you become the measuring rod. Each person has an ability to gain a relationship with the unseen as long as they trust their own knowledge, the validity of their own measuring rod.

In magick, as in life, we have competition. People try to pull out their invisible rods and compare sizes. Know that size in unimportant in magick. It is the will of your intention, and the strength of your belief that will create magickal events, and build a relationship with the unseen. I suggest not divulging every aspect of your magick when sharing it with others. This will help you to keep from comparing measuring rods, but also will help you to keep the power within the experience.

Giving away power is simple: one only need to defer to another. In all of my journeys the lesson comes back to me, echoing in my face, reverberating the need to not defer to another. Do not defer to the teacher. Do not defer to the master. *Do not defer.* Deference means to humbly submit yourself. Humility is good only if it comes from an empowered place, else wise humility is to defer, to look to another and say, "you are greater than I". In this submission one hands over all of their power, and becomes depleted. The human who is given this power will take it. We have not been trained in our society to keep balance between people, only to take advantages when they are given.

I met with a great teacher, and my expectation was to meet a great teacher. When I realized that this teacher was as great as I, I became disillusioned. It was not the teacher's doing, but my own. The teacher did not say, "expect greatly of me." But I expected greatly, and in my expectation created disappointment. I was disappointed because I thought a great teacher should be greater than I. This belief stems from internal deference, the desire to believe that I am not great enough. Once I am able to realize that I am one with all, and we all share in this magick, then I know I no longer need to be in search of someone greater. I have access to the infinite, as do you.

When you tell your stories of magick, if you have this internal desire to defer, then your stories will never measure up to what you expect others' stories to be. As you share your story in all of its entirety you will be expelling the energy embedded in the story. The story in your mind, full of energy, carries magick within your soul. The story that has been told with increasing deference loses all of its energy, and no longer carries magick within your mind. In this way you lose a bit of magick.

Knowing the Secrets

DOESN'T MAKE THEM Easy

EVERY DAY IS A CONSCIOUS DECISION

BUT THE TRUTH

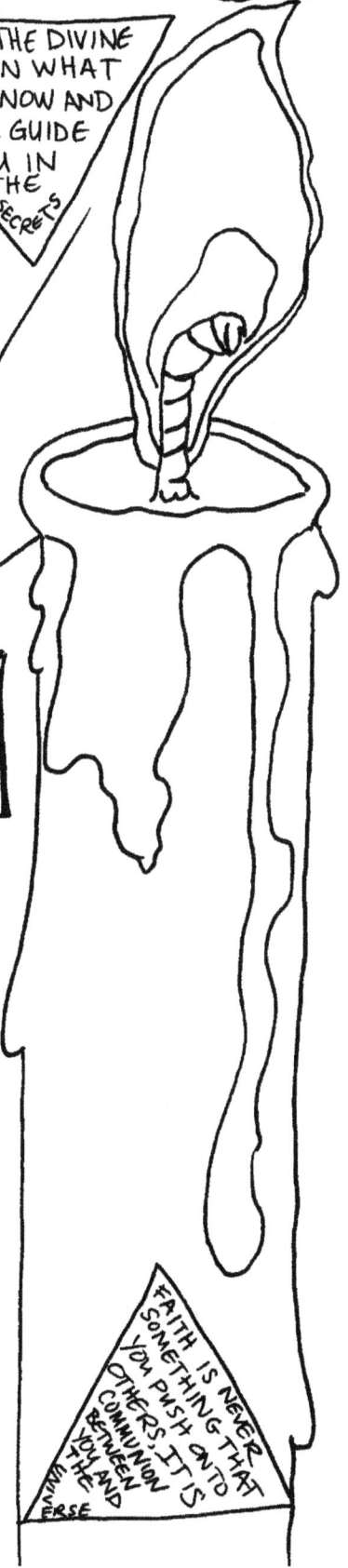

Some days you will fail

Will always GLIMMER LIGHT TO GUIDE YOU

FAITH IS NEVER SOMETHING THAT YOU PUSH ONTO OTHERS, IT IS COMMUNION BETWEEN YOU AND THE UNIVERSE

To live magick, to live the magickal lifestyle, you only need to listen with your heart to the world around you. You will not always understand. I still do not always understand. It is in the release of needing to understand all that you open yourself up to greater magick. Release yourself from expectations, take a deep breath, and be kind to yourself. This journey will give you so many gifts, and your soul will sob in the beauty of revelation. You will experience the infinite. Know that you will never own all the answers, and you will always be seeking and learning. There is no end point in the infinite.

Thank you for allowing me to open these doors for you. It is a great honor.

I call to the spirits of the East, winds of the East, great spirit bird fly with us, give me the vision to present these words with clarity, with integrity, and with understanding. Help us to see the big picture, to envision our greatest dreams, and fly towards them with willful abandon. Grant us your wings to fly on the winds of change with grace. lend us your talons to pluck out aspects of the big picture that are ready to be mulched. Connect us to the messages of great spirit, and allow us to be open and flowing like the wind, able to hear with open hearts.

I call to the spirits of the South, winds of the South, to the great serpent, come be with us. Teach us that our stories are not ourselves, but vibrations that can be shed like the skin of a snake. Teach us how to transform ourselves to our highest good. Help us to feel with our bellies and to keep strong connection with earth mother. Show us the wisdom of transformation and the power of diving deep into the core of our being. To not be afraid of the darkness, for our greatest transformation comes in blackness of a cocoon.

I call to the spirits of the west, winds of the west, to great jaguar and the rainbow bridge, come walk with us through the stories of our lives, show us how to follow the energy vibrations and see the connections between them. Teach us how to walk impeccably and courageously using all of our senses, walk by our sides and grant us the courage to mulch our heavy energy. Rainbow bridge connect us through our heart centers to the other realm, teach us how to walk with one foot in this world and one in the next.

I call to the spirits of the north, winds of the north, great spirit, hummingbird, ancestors, join us, surround us and support us with all the knowledge that has come before us. Connect us to the spark of creation, the part of ourselves that never left divine source, and quiet our minds filling us with the calm wisdom of the ages. Teach us that magick is always happening, and that we can traverse great distances by suckling from the sweetness of life. Teach us to pay attention to our surroundings, to the yearnings of our hearts and the passions deep in our souls.

Great mother earth, I call to you, support us in our journeys; remind us that we are connected to you, that we are your children, with every step that we take. Teach us the lessons of the seedling, how it grows in your soil, nurtured by your ability to transform heavy energy into food, breaking open in your safety, and reaching up to the sun. Remind us that we are connected to all of your creatures and that our brothers and sisters live in harmony with you. Teach us how to reconnect to our roots, to realize our connection, and to acknowledge the magick and beauty of your support.

To the Moon and the Sun, the stars, and all the spirit guides I call to you, walk with us on our journeys. Teach us the lessons of light, how to grow our vibrations to higher frequencies, how to see in the dark and know the moon's mysteries. Whisper your words of wisdom in our ears, and lead us towards illumination. Grant us clear visions, and clear connection to our unseen team, support our hearts energetically as we begin to open ourselves, and flourish in our healing. Remind us that we too are star people, and that our shining comes through releasing ego.

With this prayer we begin at the beginning, that you may find your heart intertwined with the mysteries once we reach the end. With love, and blessings, I welcome you aboard, and hope you enjoy the ride.

2

Beginnings:

How I came to Understand Magick

I want to weave words for you, into a little bit of a spell. I want to bring you in, and experience this with you. I want to tell you that you can talk back to gods, those mountainous energies, with their languid tongues. You can be in communion with the divine, and build an actual, reciprocal, relationship. I've always talked to gods, beginning with the Christian God. I knew him first, as a faceless father who would hold me; calm my sadness. I would talk to him at night, laying in my bed looking up at the glow-in-the-dark stars on my ceiling. I had arranged the Gemini constellation. I would tell God everything, and God always listened, and held me.

I loved Jesus too. God would hold me, but Jesus would talk to me. He would speak without words, but with the feeling in his chest. He would understand me. These two were my friends, and I envisioned them both as men. These men I carried with me. I imagine no man had a chance of impressing me, as my expectation was heavenly. Or in the very least virtuous, which is hard to come by, no matter the sex. I made my decisions with God on my side. I had no worry the repercussions of my decisions because I held each decision to word of God (and not society's view of God, but my own personal relationship). God always showed up, and Jesus would talk. Jesus and I were good friends. I could tell his purpose, and I found it to be righteous, virtuous, and definitely deviant: Jesus spoke of truth, and pointed out that though society preached his name, they rarely spoke of truth. Jesus practiced magick, and not many are ready to understand what that means. Magick is all around, and it is unnecessary to confine yourself to the title of one religion. Spirit is in all things, in all religions, and if you walk with attention, you will find the divine truth in all things.

I don't think that everyone should embark on the magickal path; I don't think everyone should be a witch. It is a lifestyle that requires one *pay attention* at all times, be sensitive to shifts, and claim personal responsibility for themselves physically, emotionally, spiritually, and mentally. There is a continuous struggle in keeping balance within yourself. A person who is not concerned with personal evolution should not engage on the magickal path as they will most likely become prey to their own dysfunctions and self-destruct.

Now, I also believe that everyone should start to become self-aware and engage in the evolution of the spirit. This is a bit like the magickal lifestyle, but without conjuring magick. Do not conjure magick if you are not ready to become self-aware. In yesteryear the shaman of the tribe would live on the outskirts of the society, was an outcast; both revered and feared. This is similarly true for the modern witch, though less so. It seems society has become so disenchanted that even the religious leaders are not feared for their abilities, but feared because of the judgment of some deity in the sky. Society doesn't really have a place for the magickal practitioner anymore, it is not a job title, and if it is, it doesn't carry the power of magick, at least in the way that it used to.

You have probably noticed how I am spelling magick. This is on purpose. I spell magick with a 'k' throughout this text to differentiate it from sleight of hand, or parlor tricks. I found this was a necessary distinction while I was working on my Master's thesis, and have kept is because I believe the distinction is important to reiterate. When I speak of magick, I am speaking of creating a manifestation on the physical realm from energies that are put out on the ethereal realm. Another way of saying this is that thoughts become things. Thoughts exist on the ethereal, they exist unseen, but still very much exist. The same is true for magickal intention, and in my opinion all magick begins as a thought. To practice magick is to put your intention into creating those thoughts. Thoughts become things already, but if you give those thoughts extra oomph then they will manifest quickly.

Expectations

There are many people in our lives who will disappoint us. Some disappoint us repeatedly. It is maddening and saddening when all we want is for those people to take into account our expectations. That's the trick! They don't know your expectations, and often they cannot live up to your expectations. I have often found that the people in our lives who constantly disappoint us are a lesson in self-knowledge. I know what I need from people, and when I come across people who cannot give me what I need I learn to accept them as they are. Expectations create disappointment. To disengage with our own expectations, we give freedom to the people in our lives to be true to who they are.

I am also aware that many times magickal experience is foreign to the new practitioner, and even sometimes to someone who has been practicing for years; it is both something they hope is real, and something they may be afraid to try for themselves. I find this to be true because if one were to try their hand at magick and have no real manifestation then logically the magick that they hoped was real becomes just another bedtime story. The fear is very real that one may be stuck in a mundane world, or, even scarier, magick does not exist. In order to quell this fear, the practitioner may refrain from ever engaging in the magickal arts; in their subconscious mind it is better to believe it is real than to find out it is not.

I understand this dynamic, and have interspersed my informational instruction in this book with stories of magick that I have experienced. These

Participation is the key

ATTENTION!

THE MORE YOU PAY ATTENTION, THE MORE THE UNIVERSE PAYS ATTENTION TO YOU

Magick happens, is happening, at every moment EVERY Moment

PAY ATTENTION

Have faith in the Mystery

stories will both familiarize you with how magick manifests (or works) as well as strengthen your hope in belief that magick actually does exist. My goal is to empower you to take many *leaps of faith* in your own life and begin on the grand adventure of your full participation in the mysteries.

I do want to say, however, that magick is real, but possibly not in the way that one would hope. Magick takes effort, and will manifest regular things: a job, a car, an opportunity. Magick does not happen without highly focused effort, and in my experience, magick doesn't manifest physical objects out of thin air. Maybe I will figure out how to do that in the future, at which point I will edit this section. Realistic expectations of what magick is will help to stave away possible disillusionment. I say this, but still fully believe I may one day learn how to fly.

I have been practicing the mystical arts since 2003, and have found that most magickal practices hold similarities in their basic premise: attention and acknowledgment of the physical world, and the energies inherent therein. It is the pursuit and exploration of these arts that has led me on the path I am on today. I love magick, and interacting with the ethereal. Embarking on this path requires attention and participation given to everyday life. I imagine if you picked up this book then you too are one of the people curious about the mysteries and magick in life. I love that the world is more magickal and mysterious than my grade school teachers ever taught me.

Take a deep breath, and open your mind. I am of the belief that all religion is bullshit, moreover all religion is completely true. If you can hang with that paradox, then you can meet me where I am! Looking at the underlying truths and lessons of each religion, one can begin to see how religion is a construct that gives a road map to the ineffable. It cannot be written down, religious experience, so it must be described and then prescribed in poetry.

Now, religion is also used as a means of social control. In pre-modern society religious belief was intertwined in the beliefs of everyday. In other words, the Shaman didn't need to control the social group, the group was already in consensus with their cosmological belief. Currently, however, religion is a tool of social control. Keep in mind, I am also a Sociologist. I would go deeper into that idea, but this is not a Sociology textbook. If you take away the social control aspects of the dominant religions, you will find morsels of spiritual mysteries plain as day. Every religion is real, with their deities and rules, and every religion is complete bullshit, with those deities and rules being spoken by a human. The mysteries are experienced differently for every person, so to write them down and say, "This is the Truth" is in itself a lie. The truth is ineffable. The Tao Te Ching gets it, "The eternal Tao cannot be spoken, the spoken Tao is not the eternal Tao" (Mitchell, 1992), and if you're down with the Tao, then you get it too, and we can stop wasting time talking about what's real or not. Everything's real, and everything's fake: live it for yourself and experience will dictate your understanding.

Beginning

It began for me as a thirst. I was parched, and I needed magick. I believed in magick from the very beginning, though it was from a state of fear. When I was seven years old my cousins decided to play a game with me called 'black magic'. I was to tell one cousin (the assistant) an object in the room and another cousin (the seer, or one who was imbued with black magic) who was at the other side of the room was to guess what I picked. It was a child's joke, as the seer would always pick the correct object due to the fact that the assistant would describe the object before mine as black. "the black chair?"

"Nope," the seer would respond absolute.

"The lamp?" the assistant would offer.

"Yes, she picked the lamp!" the seer exclaimed, and with it my utter belief that he carried 'black magic', which convinced me my cousins were working with the devil. I screamed and ran to my mother, "They're doing black magic mom!"

The cousins laughed. I believed.

My belief was always shaded in fear. At the schoolyard when kids were playing 'light as a feather', and the sky was overcast with ominous October clouds, I would stand on the edges fervently praying under my breath to Jesus, that the work of the devil would not prevail. I was so very afraid.

I was also thirsty. My prayers would follow me into the night, and throughout the day. I prayed to God to show me signs, to explain away confusion. I always asked for a sign. Once I prayed, "God, help me to understand why I am a lesbian. Show me a sign," at that exact moment, a large branch cracked and broke off the huge silver dollar eucalyptus tree in my mother's front yard. It wasn't a twig; it was a large branch! I had no idea what it meant, but I knew that God was listening. Many times the signs didn't give clarity, but brought more confusion. God was always there, but I didn't always understand. My life was filled with an enchanted mist, which I understood as God, but later interpreted as the world of magick. And if you believe that God is all, then you are right, and that is what I am saying.

The day I admitted to myself that I am gay, I lost inclusion into my enchanted understanding. I felt like I was dropped from the loving arms of

Christianity, though I still kept contact with God. God loved me, even if God's followers believed me to be living in sin. I knew my love couldn't be a sin. Soon even God would dwindle away, and my understandings were pushed open, to the point of discomfort. I questioned everything I had believed. My foundation suffered the earthquake, the instability that accompanies the beginning of the magickal path. You cannot embark on this path until you are made very uncomfortable. You have to challenge consensual reality to be able to commune with magick.

The beginning of my magickal life goes back in time to both childhood, and the realization of my sexuality. Without the consequences of these two aspects I may have never delved into the mysteries. I always believed in magick, and so diving into it was a given. Further, it is with these experiences that I was able to transition into the magickal lifestyle without the nagging fear of hell; a freedom that I realize is not universal to all mystical seekers. My sexuality had stripped me from the opportunity of heaven, so the fear of hell became less real. The quicker you can break down the foundations of your reality, the more thoroughly you can rebuild them with the mysteries.

My struggles with my sexuality led me to have to deal with breaking down the foundations of my belief early on. I was not the type of lesbian who could be out, and proud, and still follow a religious paradigm that taught me I was bad for loving someone of the same sex. Currently, this idea is losing foothold in the churches, and I am glad to see that, however, in my experience I had to choose between following my heart or continuing to give my belief to a tradition that both held women in contempt, and viewed homosexuality as an abomination. In order to accept myself I had to train my mind out of believing in eternal damnation. As I began studying Wicca I found that this transitional process I had already gone through readied me to engage with a new system. I realize that this is not an easy feat, especially if there has never been a reason to push against the dominant belief system. It can be done though, and once you free yourself from the confines of social control, you are liberated to create life in the most magickal ways possible.

I studied Wicca 101 with Cindy Gumucio. A traditional year and a day was required to become a priestess of the Goddess. A Goddess!? My brain could barely keep the thought without laughing. For such a liberal-feminist-lesbian I was sure having a difficult time acquainting myself with a female divinity. My first attempts at visualizing a Goddess turned out to be some bizarre mixture between Barbie and Jesus. I decided I wouldn't put any urgency into finding the Goddess, and instead focused on researching different mythologies. I began talking to a goddess, and the longer I talked to her, the clearer her image became in my head. Different mythologies have different goddesses, and familiarizing myself with each of their archetypes made it easier to gain their audience.

The Wicca classes were geared towards getting us all comfortable with practicing a spirituality that wasn't Christian. Through guided meditation and Goddess chants we were being gently introduced to a pagan tradition, something that most of us were a bit uncomfortable with. Coincidently, I felt that the rituals did seem very similar to church, but I tried to ignore my aversion. Spiritual practices are all very similar. If you have tension within yourself regarding one specific religious or spiritual practice you might find yourself having difficulty familiarizing yourself with another practice. Know that your bad experience in one belief system will shadow your attempts at finding another belief system because of these similarities.

I didn't immediately take to the magickal lifestyle because I thought we would start with magick, not with ritual. I wanted magick! Where was the magick? I understand the incessant desire to find out that magick is real, and how it works, because I too was driven by that hope and curiosity. I understand now that you can't start off with the magick because initiates will run off, and run amok, with their new abilities creating lots of energetic backlash. Without a basis and understanding of the world of energy, the cosmology of whatever path you are following, you will lack foundation; you will get into trouble. I do, however, like to start my students off with some folk magick in order to capture their interest while laying a foundation for new understandings of how the cosmos work.

I really didn't take to the magickal lifestyle until I realized that magick is real. Half way through our year and a day training Cindy had us do a releasing ritual, where we were allowed to write down a laundry list of all the stuff we wanted to get rid of in our lives. I wrote down in earnest the bad relationship that had never seemed to be cut clean, the odd skin growth I had recently developed and something else, that I can't remember.

When we began to open sacred space and call in the Goddess my left hand began to buzz and tingle. I had never had this sensation before and I was excited at the development. I cast my paper into the burning cauldron to begin to rid myself of all the things I no longer wanted. Then we were done and we all went home. During the next two weeks my skin growth turned black and fell off, and the bad relationship was severed, my ex-girlfriend telling me she no longer wanted to be in contact with me. All the stuff I had put on that list to get rid of was now gone! Magick worked! I was hooked.

Later in my shamanic studies I would learn how to further heal those experiences that I wanted to rid myself of, so that their energetic vibration no longer colored my outlook and reactions to people. Given my beginnings I had

Knowing yourself means looking at the parts of your story where you're not the hero, where you're ashamed to look.

LOOK THERE

Look There & forgive yourself

Apologize

MAGICK
REQUIRES
PERSONAL
RESPONSIBILITY

You know yourself now, and are responsible for your actions

Because they will happen again, but you don't get to play dumb anymore

and decide how you will approach those situations when they arise again much to heal and release. In my practice I have found that if we use magick to get rid of bad things and don't also address the root of the problem, the bad things might go away initially, but the vibration of those bad things still live in our energy fields, and will come back. In order to have a spiritual practice that benefits the practitioner, and the world, that spiritual practice must evolve. This evolution must always be concerned with healing the wounds of the spirit, and creating a balanced reality that doesn't give in to victimization. You may be a victim, but if you make that your identity you will always be a victim.

In my magickal life I have integrated both the Q'ero cosmology with my magickal training, and find that I benefit from always being open to learning a new tradition. In my experience I have found that magick is amazing and awesome, but can be debilitating without the shamanic Q'ero practices. Magick increases ones' access to power and energy, which is good, but can also make one implode if their energy body (soul) is all messed up. The Q'ero tradition focuses on healing the soul and integrating energy that allows a person to interact with the underworld, middle world, and upper world. So, in layman's terms: if you are a bundle of sadness, and trauma and you start shooting magick out into the cosmos to fix the problem, you are asking the cosmos to fix you. Getting fixed is uncomfortable. If you are not ready to be fixed, the magick will destroy you in the effort to help you fix yourself. For me, the shamanic practices are how I make sure I am energetically ready to be fixed.

One semester I was telling my students about how I've had interactions with God, and later with Hekate. One student raised his hand and asked, "So, did you reinterpret your first experience with God as being with some other deity?"

What a fascinating question! At the root of the question there is an assumption: only one religion can be true. But here's the secret: it's all true. When I prayed to Hekate it begins to rain. When I prayed to hummingbird, a hummingbird flew over my head. When I prayed to God a branch broke. When I pray, I get answers. The only logical conclusion that I can see is that all is connected. They are archetypes of the collective whole. When I pray to a Goddess I am calling on archetypal energies, but also the deity exists. Archetypes exist and resonate at a particular frequency. Deities exist and often represent archetypes. You might come to find that you, yourself, are an archetype. To align with different frequencies is to alter one's consciousness. To accept them all, is to open to the oneness of everything. A magickal tapestry that encompasses all of life, all of history.

When I was around eleven, I remember my mom telling me about how God listens to prayer. She recounted to me some ways in which miracles had happened in her life when she prayed to God. She proceeded to tell me that recently she had been low on money, and didn't have enough to pay all the bills. She was scared. She prayed. A couple of days later she found a check that she had forgotten to cash, and it was enough to allow her to pay all her bills. It was a miracle. My faith was established early, as my mom often had examples of how God worked miracles in her life. Thinking back now, I know that my own understanding of magick was based in these experiences with my mom. My mom taught me to believe, and I did. She taught me that prayer worked. Even when I left Christianity I never stopped believing in the unseen, I only had gained disillusionment about the followers, and the church. My belief is still very strong. In my experience magick is just prayer with props, and faith that it is being heard.

I believe all the magickal systems that humans have created are true, and also completely made up. *Just because something is imaginary doesn't mean it is not real.* I accept all deities because if people believe in them, then they are real. I have this idea that all thought-forms are created, and exist, if only in the minds of people. But as I've stated before, just because it is in your imagination doesn't make it unreal. The imagination is the most powerful, real tool, that humanity has.

If you can suspend the belief that you will go to hell for adopting a new deity, and giving up the monotheistic paradigm, or create a shift in consciousness (personal paradigm shifting), then you can free yourself and see the oneness in all things. Once you can allow yourself to embrace other deities and spirits, then prayer and magick are basically the same.

As an atheist or agnostic looking for a keyhole or loophole into magick I would point to Jungian archetypes and how the archetypes are universal and exist throughout humanity, and if you look at Goddesses, Gods, deities, etc., as archetypes then you can embrace or tap into the energetic resonance of that vibration and create magick utilizing it within you. Basically the idea that we are all God-heads is true, we are all personal Gods and the cosmos exist within us, and to create magick you are just shifting your cosmos. You can't shift everyone else's cosmos; you can only shift yourself. Casting magick is to bring energy through yourself and projecting it out to create change.

This is my beginning, where my path began. Your path will be different. Take what resonates, and discard the rest. Welcome to communion with the cosmos.

3

Shaman Witch, and Other Attempts at Labelling

I am a shaman witch, but that's just a label. I am a magickal, mystical, ethereal traveler, who likes to look beyond the mundane, in all that I do. Labels are useful for society: who are you, what do you do? We like to be able to categorize people, and things, so that we know how to treat them. We also like to categorize ourselves, to take on an identity. The actual use of labels, however, is problematic, as it tricks us into forgetting our own fluidity. It constrains our identity.

I call myself a witch because it is a word generally used to demean women. I personally like to utilize labels to expand people's minds, and make them question what they know. I say it proudly; I own it. I walk around claiming a title that so many people are afraid of, and I do it with a trickster's smile. I am a witch, and I'm not afraid of the backlash. I know the stories of the witch burnings, and that's not going to deter me. I'm not afraid of what the neighbors will say, I'm not afraid of losing my job. I refuse to subscribe to our culture's fear of the witch. In this way people are forced to face their own assumptions, and the ideas they were raised to believe about witches, when they interact with me.

I like to use the word shaman because I walk with one foot in this world, and one in the next. I alter my consciousness at will. People also associate maleness with the word shaman, so I am subverting their assumptions. Further, I have found some people will say 'shaman' with reverence, whereas they will say 'witch' with scorn. These revelations reveal gender norms, and the devaluation of women. Shaman and witch are basically the same, though their titles have been used at different times, and for different cultures. Sometimes I will even call myself a sorcerer. The 'sorcerer' is considered a bad-ass!

There is supposedly a difference between a witch, a shaman, and a sorcerer though I think the definition is different depending on the context and culture being referenced. I have a tendency to view all three titles as the exact same, but with different social definitions (for example witch, and sorcerer both have negative connotations in American society, whereas shaman is usually viewed positively, or with curiosity and awe).

A witch conjures, utilizes the knowledge of magick to cast spells, and interacts with magick. The shaman, which I view as a witch from yesteryear, interacts with the various worlds (Underworld, Middle world, Upper world) and utilizes the knowledge of magick to create balance in their world. The sorcerer utilizes the knowledge of magick and ritual to affect change (aka interact with magick). If I say witch to you, you probably visualized an ugly old woman. If I say shaman, you probably visualize a tribal man. If I say sorcerer you probably visualize a [sometimes sinister] old man with a big staff. It seems to me the bulk of the difference between these practitioners resides in the mind of the person hearing their name.

A witch, sorcerer, and shaman are all mystics on the path of interacting with the unseen, and fully engaging in the mysteries of life. Their lives are dedicated to working with the ethereal realms. They all engage to shift reality at will. Generally, they are all from different pantheons, or parts of the world. Shamans are associated with magick that existed before theism (because they are animists, everything is connected and has consciousness). Every culture, in every place started with shamanism. Sometimes there are sorcerers in the shamanic worldview, and in this way they are often considered evil, or engaged in power for power's sake. This, of course, is dependent on the language and translations being utilized.

The witch is also considered evil in certain parts of the world, bringing pain and plague to those whom she detests. In other parts of the world, however, the witch is merely she who would interact with magick. I say she, because there is a tendency to believe a witch is a woman, however, men are witches too. In one period of time male witches were called warlocks, but in another period of time warlock meant an 'oath breaker' or one who betrayed their coven. Personally, I think the use of the word warlock to differentiate the sexes in terms of witchcraft is a lame desire to propagate the social norms of gender division. As witches we transcend normative reality, so why this need to invoke societal normalcy in our terms? As witches, or magickal practitioners, our expression of self is fluid, and is unable to be confined by definitions.

It is also important to note that each and every title used to describe a person who practices magick will have cultural context association. So, in some parts of the world to be a witch is to be someone who casts bad magick. We must acknowledge this contextual definition when reading about other cultures, and their responses to witches. However, it is also important to point out that many times a culture will construct a negative title for an 'other' within their culture. To construct a title which will rally the masses to try and rid themselves of people is not something I find ethical, or virtuous, rather it is just a continuation of humanity's desire to enslave the masses with their adherence to norms, and 'in-groups'; to find a way of justifying hating someone.

You can probably tell that I am able to maintain various realities, that may or may not seem mutually exclusive, afloat in my mind continuously. Whether the witch, shaman, or sorcerer are good or bad people, there have been definitional distinctions between them. According to Raven Grimassi a witch [of European roots] is, "a man or a woman who is involved in magick and some form of Paganism" (Grimassi, 2000). Grimassi goes on to say, "The witch figure most likely evolved from the primitive shaman or sorcerer/sorceress character common to tribal communities." (Grimassi, 2000). Though Grimassi refers to a primitive practice, I want to state that I do not approve of the term primitive because it denotes inferiority, however, it is the term used in most anthropological studies, and so is recognized with that signifier. Grimassi goes on further to describe these characters as having the ability to interact with the various dimensions of reality. It would seem that Grimassi and I are basically in total agreement.

Though I agree with Grimassi in regards to these definitions, I also know that there are different practices associated with each of these characters. According to Greenwood & Airey (2006) the shaman is "the mediator between the everyday world and the spiritual dimension" (258), however just a few sentences later they refer to the shaman or sorcerer, and then try to define sorcery on the next page as being usually associated with evil intentions.

To define sorcerer, I choose to look towards the writings of Carlos Castaneda in his interactions with Don Juan Matus. Carlos Castaneda defined sorcery as perceiving energy directly, and sorcerers are the navigators of living energy. He goes on to say, "Sorcery is a flow, a process. Just as in physics you need certain knowledge to follow the flow of the equations" (Details magazine, 1994). I am aware that Carlos is very likely a fraud, but that doesn't detract from the truths that can be found in his writings.

As you can see, defining the differences between witches, shamans, and sorcerers is not easy, and possibly not necessary in this context. I carry both male and femaleness inside of me, I am fluid. A bridge-person. When I am around a group of witches they refer to me as 'the shaman', and when I am around shamanic practitioners they call me 'the witch'. I am both. I am a mystic, a sorcerer, a shaman, a witch, an eccentric, a pagan. Whatever. I am part of everything, as we all are. In the meantime, I like to associate myself with labels that have negative connotations that I disagree with. In this way I look to change the definitions that people hold in their minds. I am a trickster.

There is no magick without tricksters; often the door openers. Tricksters have a far reaching history within humanity. Some tricksters are malicious, while others are benevolent, but they all have one purpose: to bring change and evolution. Tricksters subvert the social norms! The norms of society function to keep things steady: social stability. These norms, however, become antiquated with the movement of time, evolution of culture, and as such they need to be questioned. Forcing people to question their subconscious allegiance to social norms is the role of the trickster. A trickster wants you to know yourself, and why you believe what you do.

Magick is reality, labels are an afterthought. You will, however, need a basic understanding of some concepts in order to walk this road with me. Words have meaning, so let's get down to some definitions. A witch is someone who casts magick, and a shaman, who by definition enters altered states of consciousness. I find that witches and shamans are not very different, except for societal expectation. In my experience it seems that witches and shaman are basically the same thing, though their cosmologies, as is true with every pantheons' cosmology, are different.

Not all Wiccans are witches. Some Wiccans will observe the Holy-days of the year (Sabbats/Esbats), and the moon cycle, but never cast a spell. I have met some Wiccans that don't believe in magick. I am both a Wiccan and a witch. My Wiccan training laid a foundation for further growth into different specialties. I would say I am more of an Italian witch, but that is mostly by ancestral memory, and lineage, not by formal teaching. What I'm going to give you in this book is not a specific training, but a culmination of the mysteries that I have found running through all that I have learned. These are what I consider the essence of magick. You can choose your own labels later.

The Sabbats/Esbats are situated on the power days, or holy days, which correspond with seasonal changes. You must familiarize yourself with the energies of the seasons, cycles, and growth to understand magick. the Sabbats, Esbats, and moon cycle are very important to understanding energy currents. The moon orbits around the earth, and reflects the sun's glow. The moon is a satellite, and yet the oceans respond to her pull. Our bodies are made up of, on average, 60% water. The brain is made up of roughly 80% water. The moon affects tides, and water. Water is associated with emotions, and the subconscious. So, when you go out and work your magick with the moon you are tapping into both physical bodies, as well as subconscious communication lines. Moon magick affects us individually, as well as the collective us. This is one aspect of the moon's mysteries, and truths. You must familiarize yourself with these cycles. Don't rely on a book verbatim; go live it, get a physical understanding of each of the mysteries, of the rhythmic patterns of life.

I talk back to gods, and spirits, regularly. I do not say this to insinuate rebellion. I am not being rebellious. Well, sometimes I am, but only in a playful way. I am having a relationship, communion, with all those unseen around me. I have given full faith and privilege to the spirit's guiding; it seems that is the only way to garner a relationship with spirit and

LABELS

Are Important To Society and Can be Useful For intention But you are Fluid, And to allow Transformation You must not be CONFINED BY LABELS

messengers. I love this life, but I can see that it is not for everyone. It can be an uncomfortable place to take residence; in constant transition, whether physically, emotionally, mentally, spiritually. If you decide this is too much, then put it down. Do not engage in the mysteries half-heartedly. Always commune, this is a must in magick.

Engaging in magick can help people out of the dark, teach them how to traverse the worlds, so that they are no longer enslaved to their sadness. It is not a given though, one must embark on the journey with a willingness to be open, to strive for the truth within themselves, for the purity of their heart. To engage in magick you must be willing to commune with the gods, with the spirits, with life unseen. In this communion you must also learn to listen. Learn to listen with a mind clear of thoughts. Learn to listen with your heart.

Magick is a desire to believe that lives in your soul, and the will to enact that lives in your blood. Plainly stated, magick is the act of etheric energy put out in the world to manifest a change. I spell magick with a 'k' to differentiate it from sleight of hand, and to remove all association with card tricks and illusion. Magick is a prayer that is answered, a message from spirit, interaction with the infinite. Magick is shifting one's consciousness, and reality, at will. I say that magick is life because in every moment the natural world is communicating, and if you engage in that communication you become aware of hidden knowledge. It is communion with the spirits that produces magick. Some may argue the nuances of this point, but so far, in my reality, spirits are the intermediary for magickal happenings.

I consider myself a shaman, witch, and sorcerer, and find no actual conflict between the titles, and further do not believe I am evil, or malicious. I have moments of anger, as we all do, but I do not cast magick from those moments, and do not suggest it. Sometimes in my rumination I imagine

Your thoughts can imprison you in Hell, or grant you passage to Heaven. You must pursue your own freedom.

SEEK OUT FREEDOM

perspective is the key

SEEK OUT Love

Heaven and Hell are available at All Times

SEEK OUT JOY AND COMPASSION IN ALL YOU DO, AND STRIVE TO INCORPORATE THOSE VIRTUES INTO YOUR PRAYERS

Do not hand over your joy to systems within society that would have you cower in fear

IT DOES NOT MATTER WHO YOU PRAY TO, ONLY THAT YOU PRAY WITH YOUR HEART OPEN

Do Not trust Those who Would fill your heart with Fear

peoples' responses to hearing that I am either a shaman, a witch, or a sorcerer, and each of those is different. Their responses empower my self-image and the power associated with that. If people are more afraid, or in awe, of a sorcerer than a shaman their responses are like gifts of energy. My subconscious gathers that and applies it, and the next time I cast magick it is informed by that awe, which gives my magick more potency. Does that make sense?

The more I practice magick, and learn about magickal traditions, the more I am aware that magick resides within the mind and consciousness; if you can trick your mind into believing it, then you can do it. The secret code to all of life is belief and it is actually very difficult to train yourself to believe something that you have been socialized to disregard, or not believe in. The sorcerer, the shaman, and the witch, all know this, and they endeavor to disconnect from consensual reality, freeing themselves from the confines of the masses they have the ability to transcend.

The underworld, middle world, upper world are conceptual understandings of the structure of reality. I have found this to be archetypically true for many different cosmologies, and so I have taken it as foundation of my belief. Even in Christianity there is heaven, earth, and hell. upper, middle, under. The underworld is not evil, though you probably have that association. The underworld can be your subconscious, the middle world your consciousness, and the Upper world your superconscious. The id, ego, and superego. The underworld is what is hidden below, and often where our trauma resides, but also where one finds power. The Middle world are our everyday experiences, and the Upper world is where the spirit soars. All three are necessary, and purposeful.

I mention the 'mysteries' many times throughout this book, and it is a term that I use to encapsulate the mysteries of life, that upon journeying the magickal path one comes into contact with. Life is a mystery, and the more you pay attention to the mysteries of life, the sooner you will be brought into their teachings, their metaphors, and ultimately understanding how magick works. When I first started out I was always asking, "But, what are the mysteries!?"

No one would give me a straight answer. They would answer, but their answers were always cryptic and super confusing. I have pondered this reality often, because as I have grown in magick, I now understand the meaning of the mysteries, and when I try to explain it to my students, I am often met with, "But, what are the mysteries!?" Now I'm the one being cryptic. So, here's an answer I've come up with:

The mysteries are aspects of life that can't be understood through the mind, only comprehended through the experience.

Emile Durkheim spoke of the sacred and the profane; the sacred being that which is imbued with magick, and the profane is everything else (Johnstone, 2007). To live the magickal lifestyle, to really begin to understand magick is to understand that there is no profane. Everything is sacred. The shaman, the witch, the sorcerer, all have one foot in the physical world, and one in the etheric world. The etheric world is laid right on top of the everyday world, and so magick is imbued in all things, always. The degree of energetic volume changes depending on the amount of focus that has been put on magick. What does that mean? Magick is in everything, but in some things it is stronger because the intention has been put there. Some places have stronger energetic output than others, and we look to those places to work more magick.

The directions and archetypes are very important to understanding one's placement within the reality. Or not. I find that the archetypes, which are different from one cosmology to the next are ways to acquaint you with the energies of the universe. The birds are about flying and being a visionary. The wind is about communication. Birds and wind are associated with the East, the Spring. The serpent is about going inward, or underworld, and shedding skin. Fire is about passion, and transformation. These are each associated with the South, the Summer. The jaguar is the tracker; it stalks its prey. Water is about emotions, and resonance. The jaguar can track your emotions to the source; jaguar can read resonance. Jaguar and water are associated with the West, the Fall. The earth connects us to what is concrete, what grows, like the roots of trees, and plants. North is the winter, is the stability of concrete reality, the Winter. These expand with your relationship with them. Get to know the patterns.

Each and every archetype is a generally defined according to the particular cosmology, to show how their world is ordered. North, East, South, West can all be associated with archetypes, and with parts of your body. Macro, micro. Everything, and I mean *everything,* has a magickal correspondence, with multiple meanings. They all interconnect. Such is the nature of magick.

Sacred space is important in that you need to learn how to create a space that is separate from your everyday reality. This helps focus your intent and your magick. We all become hypnotized by the mundaneness of everyday interactions, that we forget that magick is always happening. By creating sacred space, you are engaging your magickal side. You are also setting boundaries. I like to imagine it as water boiling. Boiling water in a smaller pot will be faster than a larger pot. By setting your sacred space in magick you are setting boundaries of a smaller pot so that you can heat it up faster, and more effectively. Only those invited in will be allowed to enter. You must be clear with your boundaries, both spiritually and mundanely.

From this point what you call yourself is not important. You can take on any label that fills your heart, and live as that. It does not matter. All that matters is that you concern yourself with the greater truths of life, the mysteries that can only be experienced by the individual, alone. You can practice *any* religion, or spiritual practice, and experience the divine. Allow your spirit that experience, and that journey.

4

Spirits Guiding

Listening to the spirits guide you is one of the most important tools you have in your magickal toolbox. In order to listen to the spirits, you must believe that they are talking to you, and not think that it is just your imagination. Further you must pay attention. I have seen so many people just not paying attention, completely unaware that magick is happening all around them and that the spirits are trying to guide them. Paulo Coelho said in *The Alchemist*, "The universe conspires to help you." (Coelho, 1993). You do also have the choice whether or not to listen to them. Listening to the spirits is a practice that you hone over time, so in the beginning be sure to both listen, and pay attention to your feelings. If you hear a spirit telling you things, but you feel angry, jealous, insecure, or otherwise 'feel bad', then don't listen! You are always in control of your actions.

Clear your mind, and listen. It's as simple as that. Listen, the spirits are guiding you, they are helping you and they are revealing the truth to you. Sometimes the real reason we don't listen is because we don't want to face up to the truth. We don't want to know that we shouldn't be in a relationship (we already know, and we are living in blissful ignorance!... well, not blissful really), or that our decision is a poor one, or that so-and-so is lying to us. So we ignore the spirits and find out the hard way later, as we curse ourselves saying, "I knew it! I knew it from the beginning! Why didn't I listen?"

Sound familiar? Yeah, well, you're not the only one. Many people do it. I had a difficult time learning how to listen to the spirits too. I would constantly tell myself that other people were more intuitive than me, and I would defer to their visions and devalue my own. This is a hard lesson to learn, and it may take years. Your guides tell you what you need to hear, and they will tell you more if you believe them and are listening. Further, your guides and other people's guides may not say the same thing. Always trust

Every Thing Has Spirit, Listen with your Heart

WHEN YOU LISTEN TO THE SPIRIT, YOU MAY FIND A KINSHIP WHEREIN THAT BEING WILL BE AN ALLY.

TRUST YOUR HEART

MEET THE SPIRIT OF ALL THINGS WITH YOUR SPIRIT, AND WHERE THE TWO COMBINE IS THE HOLY COMMUNION

SOMETIMES THE SPIRIT OF A HUMAN WILL NOT MATCH THEIR WORDS, OR ACTIONS. TRUST WHAT YOU KNOW, BUT REALIZE THEY ARE UNAWARE OF THEMSELVES.

your guides, they give you the truth that is for you. Everyone is on a different journey, so guides may not always agree. Their guides are teaching them lessons, just as yours are, so do not defer to someone else's truth despite your own.

The spirits speak in many ways: thoughts in your head, pictures in your head (inner-eye visions), a high-pitched buzzing sound, or even visions outside of your inner-eye. Sometimes they are giving you information, and sometimes they are warning you. I have had many of these experiences, and by sharing them with you possibly they will resonate and help you to trust your own guides.

Vision: A few years back I had decided to go hiking in a nearby canyon with a close friend of mine, who is also psychic. We drove the curvy road to the entrance, and prepared to possibly gather sage or Mugwort. As we walked through the gate where the trail began we both walked about ten feet and stopped, almost in unison. I looked around in a sort of haze, and she asked me, "Do you feel that too? Are we supposed to be here?"

I didn't immediately want to say that I thought it felt like we should leave because the car ride there had taken about an hour, and I didn't much like not having accomplished anything in our trip. But the more I felt the energy, the more I had to agree that it did not feel like we should take our hike.

"I think we should go," I replied.

"Me too."

As we turned to leave the trail I gasp and jumped back what seemed to be ten feet! Clear as day I was looking at a huge mountain lion eating something meaty on the ground about twenty feet ahead. My gasp and terror filled the space inside my head, as I thought, "Holy shit! This is how it ends!?"

THE SIGNS ARE THERE ON PURPOSE

Learn to Read Them

By looking into metaphors, and trusting the intrinsic Feelings in your guts, in your bones. YOU Always Have access to the

Truth

ALWAYS

It was so clear, it was so outside of my head, it was right there in front of me, and then it was a boulder. "What the fuck!?" I exclaimed.

"You see it too?" she replied, surprised that we were sharing a vision.

"That rock was a huge mountain lion eating something," I answer, my voice still shaking.

"I saw the mountain lion in the tree, right there," she said, pointing at a tree not far from the rock, "I guess we listened correctly, we are not supposed to stay here!"

"I guess so, "I said, and scurried back towards the car.

Visions outside of your mind, or what you see that turns out the 'not actually' be there (though it really is there ethereally), are a way in which the spirits will guide you. You will not always have hallucinatory visions, but if/when they come, and especially when unaided by a teacher plant, it is a means to really grab your attention. Mere whispers will not do because the message is urgent. I don't have hallucinatory visions all the time, but I trust them when they come in. Do not judge yourself or your magick if you haven't had any visions. You have a long life to live, there is time.

Visions come in many forms, you may begin to see energy emanating off of human beings, animals, or plants. Some people will explain it away as being tired, or having blurry vision, "You need glasses!" Pay them no mind, and pay attention to the new sight that you are developing. You do not have to share it with everyone, and in fact you may find there are precious few people who can share in your journey. When you see things, your first thought will be, "What does that mean?" Your answer will come from the feelings that accompany the vision. There are many books out there that you can use for reference, but again, you need to trust your own intuition, your own feelings, your own guides.

I have had visions that were not urgent so much as informative. Less urgency, but still important that I pay attention. These tend to be thought visions instead of external visions, or visions in your mind's eye. More than any other types of visions, people tend to brush these off as their imagination. With time, practice, and patience, you will be able to train yourself to know the difference between imagination and mind's eye visions.

Visions in your mind's eye, or inner eye vision: Working magick and living the magickal lifestyle requires you to become aware, and to pay attention. Not only must you be conscious of the unspoken energies that people are carrying, but you must also be aware of visions in your inner eye, or third eye. There are different ways to have inner-eye visions; you can receive a vision with your eyes closed that seems so real you believe that your eyes must be open, you may have a feeling and a sensation when looking at something with your eyes closed, or you can specifically ask the universe, or your guides, to give you information on something and you receive a scene playing out in your mind, like a memory. This memory, however, doesn't always come through as something you've experienced, and sometimes it does. I have had inner-eye visions where my guides show me a memory of my own to convey the feelings experienced by the person I am inquiring about, other times I see clearly in my mind a memory or situation that isn't mine.

One experience of an inner eye vision that I had, that was like having my eyes open, was when I was just falling asleep. Come to think of it, most of these types of visions come to me at that time. I saw a spider come into focus, and it was weaving its web. It was weaving, and weaving, and it looked like I was watching an actual spider. The message, for me, was to create my life, or

LISTEN TO THE GUIDANCE OF THE SPIRITS

DREAMS

They will communicate through signs, feelings, echoes, and sometimes direct expression

If you are not willing to listen, do not ask.

If you ask for advisement be willing to listen to it.

No matter how much you've got your Heart set on something, if the Spirits warn against it, do not pursue.

UNLESS YOU KNOW THAT YOU MUST GO FORWARD INTO THE LESSON >> THEN BE SURE TO TRY TO LEARN WITH COMPASSION.

to continue to create my life. It was also a reminder that we can weave our realities into existence in the dream time.

Close your eyes and imagine the room you are sitting in; your mind would probably first reproduce the scene from memory. If you spend a little more time, and 'look' around the room with your eyes still closed you may begin to feel things at certain parts of the room, or see things. This type of vision allows you to see spirits or messages that are always there, but not loud enough to be a full on vision. You can train yourself to see inner eye visions with your eyes open, and often when psychics are telling you what they are seeing, it looks as if they are having a hallucinatory vision right in front of you, but actually they are having an inner eye vision. With training this will become stronger, and as with anything, some people are born with stronger proclivities towards one gift or another. Don't judge yourself based on your perceptions of others.

When you are practicing your inner eye vision you may notice a cat you had years ago pop up, or grandma sitting on your couch. I find that your immediate guides are both familiar, and less scary than spirits you haven't met before, especially when you are just starting out. This is normal, and when you see grandma I want you to have a conversation with her, in your mind. You ask a question, and then wait for a response. The way that you know it is not your imagination will be the specific feeling that you get with her response. Sometimes, when I am speaking to my Nana, she will say something that has just the right amount of humor, and it will kind of jolt me, and make me laugh. I didn't expect it. If you are getting responses like, "I love you" that don't surprise you, then you must keep asking questions. Look for a response that makes you feel something you weren't expecting, and then remember that feeling.

THE TRICKSTER IS SOMETIMES CONSIDERED THE CULTURE HERO TURNING NORMS ON THEIR HEAD AND BRINGING EVOLUTION

TRICKERY

some times you must be tricked into learning your lessons.

SOMETIMES TRICKERY IS THE ONLY WAY FOR THE TRUTH TO BE HEARD.

That feeling is often how you will know that you are actually talking to the spirits, actually having a vision.

Of all the ways in which spirit guides me, the high pitched ringing in the ear is the most confusing. I still don't have a complete grasp of it. Some people have said, "When you hear that ringing, you need to shift your vibration to the resonance of the ring, and then you will hear the words."

This is a sound theory, but I have yet to successfully shift my vibration in a way that allowed me to hear the words over the ringing. I have decided, for the time being, that a high pitched ringing means that I need to pay attention, both to what I'm saying, and what is being said. I also categorize it as a grab for attention.

High pitched ringing: This is the funniest of the spirit nudges, if only because when trying to tell non-magickal people what you're experiencing they always try to diagnose you with an ear disorder. One such occurrence happened to me when I was hiking with some friends through the Angeles National Forest. Going up a steep incline I decided to take a moment to catch my breath, and in that moment I heard the high pitched ringing. I looked around in that hazy sort of way, and my friend, who had become keenly aware of when I was getting messages, asked me what I was hearing.

"A high pitched ringing; something here wants to get my attention," I replied.

"That's tinnitus! You should get that checked by a doctor," inserted the friend of a friend, who I didn't really know.

"No, it's something trying to get my attention," I say, while reaching out to the tree that we were standing by, "Yep, it was this tree. The buzzing stopped as soon as I touched her. She just wanted me to connect with her."

My friend understood, but the friend of a friend seemed to be in new

There are multiple Realities. The Reality that is Socially acceptable is considered TruTH. These truths change over Time. To engage with the ineffable you must KNOW THIS

Perception

territory. I imagine she had not come into contact with spiritual people who would stand up to her. This brings me to another point that I need to make very clear, don't discount your experiences because science-minded people don't believe. *I have found that spiritual experiences actually follow science,* if you know the right science. Spiritual phenomena are able to be measured, tested, and explained scientifically in the right context. It takes a lot of energy to do that though, and many of us just don't care enough to explain to the cynics; so they live without magick, no skin off my ass!

Another way to listen to spirit guiding you is to ask spirit to show you a sign, and then to pay attention to the wildlife around you. To give you an example: I was driving through a canyon in Rancho Santa Margarita on my lunch break years ago, and had a question in mind for the universe to help clarify. I asked the universe to show me a sign, and then continued driving. I drove all the way through the canyon and then turned around to go back to work. I kept my eyes on the road, but opened myself to be paying attention.

As I came around one of the last corners I saw a huge bird. A super large, wings outstretched, "holy mother, what is that?" kind of bird. I pulled off to the side of the road so that I could marvel at the sight. As I looked up at it and reached my hands to the sky the bird turns its head, and then itself, so that it flew right over me. It landed on a tree across the road from my car. I stared at it in awe, not having any idea what kind of bird it was. It was golden brown, and large. Suddenly there were two Ravens flying out of a neighboring tree, headed straight for it, seemingly trying to scare it away. I watched this scene unfold and realized: I am getting my sign. Next, a Red-Tail Hawk begins to circle this same tree, screeching. I knew I was witnessing spirit's answer, and took it in for just a little while longer before needing to get back to work.

When I got back to my desk I looked up 'golden brown big bird' to see what that bird was, and to my surprise I found it was a golden eagle. As soon as the realization occurred, a calm came over me, as I understood the answer that the universe had given me. Spirit always answers, you must sit with the sign to realize its meaning.

Listening to spirits includes deities, if you believe in deities. Actually, it doesn't really matter if you believe or not. I've had archangels make contact even though I didn't really believe in angels. Similarly contact from various deities does happen, especially if they like your vibe. We do not own the spirits. The spirits have their own agency, and desires. If they want to work with someone who is outside of their cultural lineage, they will. Period. The idea that we control the spirits is a perception that comes from domination.

A society that proposes domination as a value is going to see this manifestation in their spirit work. It is a way to work with the spirits, but it's not a way that I am suggesting, nor do I think it brings about spiritual evolution. I don't like to feel dominated, and will be resentful if I am. The spirits I work with respond similarly. I keep going back to this idea that was put forth in the movie Stardust (2007), wherein the storyline follows that if you have a star's heart (they become embodied when they fall to earth), you will be immortal. The bad witch character has interpreted this to mean that she must find the star and cut her heart out of her chest. At the end we find out that the protagonist, who falls in love with the star, receives her love (or heart) in return. He becomes immortal. This idea of different interpretations of meaning having validity is important to me. The spirits can, and will, be interacted with, however, the ways in which you interact with them is indicative of what you value, and your morals.

Interacting with the spirits will magnify your motivations and actions.

This means that when you invite the spirits to interact with your life your life energy force will magnify, and the manifestations of your thoughts and feelings will augment. Having a large energy field of domination may be something that people want to strive for. I am not one of those people. I don't think domination is beneficial for your life's joy and happiness. In contrast I believe in working with the spirits with reciprocity. Respect that you would give to your grandparents, your professors, is also a way to interact with the spirit world. If you look at the foundation of most religious traditions you see that kindness, love, respect are virtues to strive for.

People may disagree with this idea. I have heard the adage, "I bow to no one, not even gods." While this may have a purpose, I immediately think of Namaste, or 'the divine light in me bows to the divine light in you". Bowing is not a show of weakness, but a testament to one's strength. Having the fortitude to bow in reverence of life is a virtue, and the sign of a true warrior. If you choose not to bow to anything, it makes me wonder what you are actually trying to say.

Trickster spirits also exist. There are various forms of trickery, and as a trickster myself, I understand trickery as a way of conveying information that would not be grasped through conventional methods. Or as Don Juan Matus tricked Carlos Castaneda into living a sorcerer's life, he knew that one must be tricked into the path, because who, in their right mind, would choose it!?

Sometimes tricksters are malevolent, which I am not fond of. These tricksters, however, still have a purpose. Tricksters, in all forms, seem to be a means of bringing about change that needs to occur, through indirect means. They trick you into the right path. Often tricksters also are the recipients of trickery. I know that my deepest lessons have come by being tricked into them. Be aware that some spirits are archetypical tricksters, and if you work with them, you will find yourself going into a lesson through the back door. They are not inherently bad, and you will get what you ask for, but don't be surprised if you fall on your ass whilst getting there.

I will state again, I have had interactions with God, and I have had interactions with Hekate (and other spirits as well, but I feel the juxtaposition of these two illustrates my point nicely). I did not reinterpret my interactions with God after the fact as being some form of a pagan deity, because at the time I believed in God, and had interaction with God. What I gained from these experiences is that *what you believe in, what you have faith in, exists.* You create your world with your words and your belief.

Listening to the Spirits Exercise:

In order to train yourself to listen to the spirits, you must begin to talk to the spirits. You can do this in your mind, and not aloud if you are worried about being perceived as crazy. Go out to a nature area. This could be your garden, or the local park. Make yourself comfortable, and then start talking to spirit. It may be best to do this in your mind at first, or if you want to do it out loud, but are self-conscious, you can wear a blue-tooth. Ask the spirits for the answer to a question. Then, pay attention, and write it down.

Write down all the natural occurrences that catch your eye during the rest of the day. Did an animal cross your path in a rather peculiar way? Write it down. You may not understand what spirit is trying to tell you, but you will later. Did a song pop into your head, on repeat? What are the words to the song? These are important details. Write it down.

5

Magick

I love magick. Magick is the foremost reason that I started studying Wicca. Magick is the golden sparkle that lights upon the edges of reality, making everything much more interesting, and intricate. I don't work magick because I want to control others, or the cosmos, but because interacting with magick is like learning how to play music. Every vibration that is utilized to work a spell, the burning candle, the incense, the intention, all come together to become a song, and each song is different. As I have become better at making magick I find that every day is a foray into the symphony of life; magick allows me to join in.

Magick is not easy, and yet it is very simple. In order to change your life you must both put out the energy of your intentions, and then also put into action the changes inside yourself in order to achieve those goals. Magick will shift energy, but if you do not deal with your issues at a core level, the changes you make will inevitably change back. I was once asked, "If you know how to do magick, why can't you just use it to change your weight?"

The question is simple and straight forward, and I could utilize magick techniques to cast a spell on myself to be the weight I desire, but without getting to the root of why I am always at a certain weight, I will not be able to have lasting effects. Now this is not always true. Sometimes with the magick I have cast, the spell has been so powerful and pure that the intent manifested within me and changed my actions without me even really trying. Eventually, however, the thought to engage in that old behavior would surface, and in that moment I had to make the conscious decision to not go back to old patterns. If I had healed that pattern at its root, then the thought would never enter my mind. Slipping in to old patterns happened often early on in my magickal practice, and as I developed my skill, so too did I learn it will ★ **IN ORDER FOR MAGICK TO WORK** YOU MUST RELEASE IT INTO THE COSMOS, AND LET IT GO.

not be easy ★

SEEK OUT THE ESSENCE OF ALL THINGS FOR YOURSELF, MAKE YOUR OWN DECISIONS, AND FIND OUT THE TRUTH FOR YOURSELF.

Magick

a magickal journey starts with much difficulty, you must prove your self.

IS A

DO NOT BELIEVE THE DOGMA OF DOMINANT RELIGIONS, THEY SEEK TO KEEP THE MASSES IN IGNORANCE

A Witch shifts her

consciousness at will

MANA IS ACQUIRED THROUGH YOUR JOURNEY.

Lifetime

Magick requires strength, and responsibility ★

MANA IS ETHEREAL ENERGY

at the beginning it will seem as if you are always receiving riddles, but as you develop they will become clear.

IF YOU ARE AFRAID THEN YOU ARE NOT ABLE TO MOVE DEEPER INTO THE MYSTERIES

ENDEAVOR

MAGICK IS NEITHER GOOD NOR BAD BUT A REALITY OF CONSCIOUSNESS. KEEP IT PURE.

as you progress you will be better able to handle the tests ★

YOU DO NOT MASTER IT, You Engage it. →

DO NOT ALLOW PATRIARCHY IN YOUR MAGICK

SOME SYMBOLS ARE MADE TO BOTH SCARE YOU AND TEACH YOU GREATER MYSTERIES.

Those who seek power to become masters over nature and others, are devoured by their greed.

how to have a lasting effect.

Magick is real. People who meet me and learn about what I do, who are not magickal, always ask me about magick, and if it's real. As soon as I tell them that it is they immediately ask for a story that will *prove* it to them. There is difficulty with this! First of all, you cannot really explain a magickal experience to a non-magickal person without them having some understanding of magick (which is totally a paradox!). Let me give you an example. Have I told you the story about the time I was on the TV show Panic Button? Well, here it goes: I was on Panic Button, where I was made to face my fears: Spiders! I decided to view it as a shamanic initiation, and took on that perspective. In the final test there were over a dozen tarantulas dropped on my head. I conquered my fear, we won the show, and were awarded travel certificates.

When I found the time to use my certificate, I met Alessandra Belloni. She told me she was leading a group to Italy to learn the Tarantella, a shamanic drumming technique that heals the wounds of love. The travel money was perfect for the flight and lodging. Do you know what Tarantella means in Italian? Tarantula. I have told this story to many people, but only a handful of them actually recognized the magick. This is how magick works. It leads you on a journey that isn't necessarily literal, and reminds you constantly that magick is happening all the time and that it is all around. Oh! A when I returned from Italy I had this overwhelming sensation of remembrance come over my body: Many years ago I had asked the universe to get me to Italy, but I didn't want to go unless it would be magick, and I could work with a magickal practitioner.

Secondly, asking someone to prove their magick is like issuing a challenge. I always feel as if I am suddenly involved in a pissing match where my personal experiences with magick are about to be judged as amazing, or just mediocre, which is a reflection on me. Non-magickal people don't realize this because they are coming from a perspective of judging magick, and its existence, not the practitioner and their ability. Living the magickal lifestyle is an ongoing pilgrimage into the mysteries of life, and my experiences with magick when I first started off on this path are much smaller than what I've experienced now, or what I will experience in the future.

Now, I do know that non-magickal people asking me to tell them a story of the magick I've experienced is actually their way of asking for proof, so that they might believe. That I can give them faith. I understand that they want something extraordinary to believe in, and it is this knowledge that softens my response. I have experienced magick, some of which I directly conjured, and others of which were just the magickal unfolding of the spirits interacting with my life. As I write this I am struck with the idea that one of the important tenets of the magickal lifestyle is to let go of control. Magick will manifest in a myriad of beautiful, magnetic, and resounding ways; you just need to pay attention.

Living the magickal lifestyle is a choice, a decision to allow the odd quirks of the universe to interplay with your reality. In my opinion not everyone should engage in the magickal lifestyle; it is a lifetime commitment to not taking the easy road. You must know yourself, even the parts you do not like, and must strive for continuous evolution of the spirit. I am also of the belief that one only need believe in the energies of the ethereal world for the interaction to begin. So, for those who wish to begin to explore the magickal reality of the universe, know that belief will require you to pay attention to things that the mundane world will consider mere coincidence. This is the burden you must carry as a magickal practitioner, the norm of

Engage Magick

Sometimes I did not cast magick, but only spoke up, called attention of the gods to a wrongdoing, and Magick presented ITSELF

To engage magick you engage with all the spirits respectfully and show them that you pay attention. You must strive to show respect in your practice in all ways.

You will find the spirits have humor and personality.

society will not accept you, you are rare, and you are sensitive. This is not to say that the norm of society is wrong. Social norms keep in order the complexity of social interaction. It is required for one to be brave enough to go against the norm in order to endeavor on a magickal path. If this is your calling, I suspect you will read on.

I have had far too many experiences of magick happening right before my eyes, to doubt its existence any longer. I used to doubt. I grew up in America, therefore I was raised to always be looking for explanations. Interestingly I have found that most people, including my earlier self, declare that they do not believe in magick because they are logical. Magick is considered illogical. The newly exposed magical seeker usually questions, and tries to deconstruct every aspect of magick. If they create magick, and it happens, almost always a new initiate will say, "Well, it could have been because of [insert logical explanation for why your magick worked, as a means of disproving magick is real, here]". You can fill in the blank. We are taught to question, and also we are taught to forgo our power, and so the first inkling of realizing we do have power is immediately surrendered.

Every spell that I have cast, that worked, was immediately scrutinized and evaluated for its causality. Could it have been just a chance occasion? Could it have been outside variables having affect? I look back now, and often laugh at myself. It's even funnier to have new students, and watch them go through this same process; I cannot circumvent it, they must walk the path to the end. I do try to explain this all, as a means of maybe shortening their journey, but I don't think my explanations work; it seems experience is the only road to full comprehension.

Magick actually does follow logic, or valid reasoning, and that's the funniest part about it. There are actions and consequences, and a logical equational flow of how magick works. Once you finally train your mind to stop questioning the rules of magick, the logic of its working become clear and understandable. Until then, the act of questioning actually lessens the energetic output and dampens the ability of magick to happen. So, you must have faith; funny that the concept of faith transcends many belief systems. For magick to work, you must have faith that magick works, and then you can experience it.

After my final initiation into Wicca, wherein I was officially a priestess of the Goddess, I got in my car and drove to Santa Cruz; I had been accepted as a transfer student to complete my undergraduate education in the Fall. During the two years that I was at UCSC I was also a solitary practitioner, and then a witch's apprentice. I returned back to Orange County in 2007, and asked Cindy to initiate me as a High Priestess. It was awesome! I dedicated myself to Aradia, Diana and Hekate, as both a form of the triple Goddess as well as the epitome of the energies I would carry on my mystical journey. We stayed up all night, drank wine and frolicked naked under the moon on July 7, 2007 (7/7/7) to do the rite. It was magickal for both of us.

On August 13, 2007, I had a very surreal experience. I was living in Anaheim, CA, in an apartment next to my closest friends. We were up talking when I noticed the neighbor's cat, a grey and white tabby, walking across the way with a bird in its mouth. Something in me took over, and I ran after the cat, which was actually quite the opposite of what I would normally do (generally I would have stared in horror, and been quite immobile). While running after the tabby he dropped the white bird. I had never held a bird before, so I wasn't sure how to pick it up, but since the cat was turning back to reclaim his prize I had to act fast. Picking up a bird for the first time is a very special experience, as birds are interesting creatures that have a whole set of norms and rules of engagement with humans! I knew none of these rules, so I was scared, but focused on saving the bird. I brought the bird to my apartment, shut the door, and brought it into my bathroom. Not sure what to do, I set it in the tub, with the lights off so that it would be in an enclosed space, and feel safe enough to calm itself. As the bird was in the tub I could feel its terror pulsating through its core. I began to run healing energy through its body, and then felt the need to sing to it. As I sang I felt the fear, as if I was the bird, and experienced the trauma of being snatched in the jaws of a cat. I began to cry. I sang and cried, and the bird looked at me, tilted its head and seemed to ask the question, "What is this human doing!?"

Having calmed both myself, and the bird, my good friends brought over the name and number of a bird lady, someone they knew who specialized in helping hurt birds. I had resolved to bring the bird to her in the morning. I put the white bird in a box by my bed, with a towel and water. I hadn't been sleeping well in the nights prior to this experience, but that night I slept amazingly! I did get up in the middle of the night to check on the bird and make sure it was still alive, but still the sleep I experienced that night was rejuvenating.

The next morning, I opened the box to see how my little white bird was fairing, and an amazing thing happened: it flew out of the box and landed on a fairy doll I had hanging up in my apartment. I looked it in the eyes, as if to ask, "Are you ok? Are you ready to fly home?"

I swear to you the bird had a sly smile in its eyes. I reached up to get the bird from the fairy, and it flew to a broom I had hanging over my front door. I grabbed the broom carefully, and opened the door. The cat was there waiting! I immediately shut the door, and looked at the bird, "You're going to have to fly fast. That cat is waiting for you, so you have one chance."

I opened the door again, broom in hand, and directed it towards a tree one street over. The bird took flight, and I watched as it landed on that tree, far enough away to be out of danger. What a spectacular morning it was! I still had to go to work, so I readied myself and hit the road. Once I arrived at my office, I logged on to the computer and looked up 'white bird' to see exactly what kind of bird I had been interacting with. As I scrolled through the pictures, one by one, I got excited to see the one I recognized. I clicked through the picture to the website, and see what it was called: white dove. White Dove! Holy, holy, holy! With this revelation I could barely contain my excitement, what an awesome omen. Out of curiosity I began looking up the date August 13, to see if there may be any sort of symbolic meaning. Shock is a word that best describes, and yet does not describe, the complexity of the emotion that engulfed me next. August 13 is Aradia's birthday, the festival of Diana, and the feast of Hekate; the three Goddesses that I had just dedicated myself to. I knew in that moment that I had been accepted. A surreal feeling of magick and hope filled me, and stayed with me, for the rest of that month.

Magick is happening all around you, and once you learn to engage that magick and yourself, the world becomes a mystical adventure. In my experience, magick generally takes you on a journey, and reveals itself in a way that is like lightning opening your head to the unending cosmos. Everything is interconnected, entwined, and pulsing together. When you feel that sensation you know what magick is, and that it is always at work.

Spells

I do not do spells by recipe. Not everyone will agree with me on this, but it is one of my core practices. I can follow a recipe, but I find it is much more powerful (and evolutionary for your spirit, and connection to the spirits) to create magick in the moment that you are doing magick. Co-create with the cosmos, connect to your intuition and follow the lead of what feels right. Now, you probably want to have a little bit of a background in herbs, oils, candles, and other magickal techniques, but once you've got the basics down stop cooking by recipe. Create your own recipes. When you create your own magick you are engaging the emotion, and the feeling of a spell. You are allowing yourself to fully participate in the creation of magick: mentally, physically, spiritually, and emotionally. Doing instructional magick tends to engage your left-brain, and disconnects you from the feeling of magick. You can always feel it when you are paying attention.

The way I work spells isn't necessarily a long process. There are times when you will need to do very involved, time consuming spells. For the most part though, my spells are comprised of some basic elements: intention, focus, energize, and release. Using these I do any number of different types of spells. I've made vision boards on pillar candles, hummingbird feeders decorated with magickal intention, created chants, planted seeds, and on and on. Once you understand the premise, then your magick is only confined by what you can imagine.

Intention is what you bring to the table. What is it that you want to create, or change? When you write down what you want, you then must ask yourself why you don't have it yet. Many times we stand in the way of our success, our healing, because we don't know any better. We were taught through experience to embrace our ineptitude. Now, what is at the root of that, can you acknowledge that trauma, that false identity, and hold it like a baby. Re-parent it through your acknowledgment, and then embody the attitude, or energetic vibration of what you want. This is the ground work, once you complete this you are mentally ready, and your intention is defined.

Feel the Resonance of Life, observe the Rhythms. True Power comes from Being in Flow with all that is.

Focus is the act of bringing all of your attention to the ground work you just completed. When I was creating a vision board candle, as I pasted the pictures onto my candle I was working through my ground work, focusing it into my candle. You must focus your intention into the working you are doing. Sometimes, as you are focusing, you will come upon a snag. Something will take your attention. This is important! Anything that takes your attention while you're doing magick, is asking you to work through it first. Many times this is an underlying memory, or belief system, that is holding you down. You acknowledge it, and incorporate it into the magick you are working. If you can't stay focused on your magick while you are doing your magick, then it is not the right time. You will need to try again later. Focus your attention on the issues that won't let you focus on your magick.

Energizing your magick is probably my favorite part. This is where you raise the energy into the intention. You can chant, dance, sing, flail, whatever you need to do in order to have a full body experience with your magick. Without energizing your magick, it goes nowhere. Sometimes saying a prayer feels so in touch with the spirit that it feels like I am not in my body saying the prayer; this is also a form of energizing. In candle magick, the flame and the melting wax, is the energy. Candles will burn down at variable speeds, and that is the rate of energetic expulsion. You spell is like a point in space, and it takes the energy to send it, spiraling out, to the cosmos.

Release is the final step in the spell process, and possibly the most difficult. Release has two components: you must let go of the energy after you've raised the vibrations. Like a rubber band, it only shoots out if you let go. I've been in group magickal settings where we were working a ritual, but then no one was releasing the energy. We were stewing in it, and it was

The Crossroads Looks Different to every Traveller

When you have a choice to make, life presents the crossroads. When you have made a choice, you must invoke them yourself.

turning sour. It was a very memorable experience, and one the solidified the importance of letting go. Second, you must forget you did magick, or at least don't think about it. Early on in my magickal practices, I could not release. I would think, and think, and think, about every spell. Thoughts about the spell, after it has been cast, tether to the original spell work, and diminishes its focus. These spells are almost guaranteed not to work.

With these steps you will be able to work in communion with the cosmos to co-create your reality. Spell is work is very similar to prayers. I have not actually been able to find a real difference at the root of both systems, they just come from different pantheons of spiritual practice. I love doing spells because I feel like I am creating paintings with the spirit.

Crossroads

Crossroads are an important archetype that is found in the collective consciousness of all of humanity. Coming upon a fork in the road is always a moment where one asks themselves, "Which way do I go?" It is impossible to continue on the same path, as that way no longer exists. Going backwards is an option, but not recommended. The journey has led to a decision, and life will be different afterwards.

Poets have written of taking the unworn path (i.e. going on their own way, and not the way of social expectation), musicians have sung about going down to the crossroads, and many have been fascinated by the idea of trying to make a decision that is connected with the unknown. In magick the crossroads has a few different meanings: it is a place where magick is cast, as it continues to hold the archetype of changing directions, and it is also a place where the worlds meet (a bridge connecting this world to the otherworld). In both of these understandings we begin to see the crossroads as not just a

THE Smolder Burn that catches in your Throat wallows like little pools in your Eyes

is where you venture forth and in the best way possible meet yourself

This

The crossroads is a scary place

MAGICK

COURAGE Happens

is a surrender from within, to stand strong without.

place where one decides to take 'the road less travelled' but rather a place where the practitioner, with the assistance of their spirits and ancestors, decide to change their path, and their reality. The crossroads is literally where we see the convergence of directions. People drive, or travel, towards their destination, and when there comes a crossroads it is accompanied by stop signs. People travel through literal crossroads all the time, and when a crossroads appears signage must be employed in order to avoid collisions. This energy of people coming and going in many directions is held at a crossroads, and such it is imbued with the power of many energies converging.

Almost every magickal tradition that I am aware of acknowledges crossroads and utilizes the archetype. Crossroads are important if you want to change the trajectory of your life. Sometimes the crossroad will present itself, and you will be faced with a decision that you must make in order to continue forward. Other times, however, you will want to change your path before a crossroad presents itself, and it is in this way that you will need to invoke the energy of the crossroad. This is magick, changing your life before it changes itself, thereby putting you in the position of power, instead of powerlessness.

To invoke a crossroads is to decide that you want to change the direction of your path, and to do so you merely need to draw a crossroads and use it in your spell. I want to be very clear that crossroads will present themselves in your life without you invoking them, and it is a matter of personal preference whether you choose to wait for that to happen on its own. When the crossroads energy presents itself in someone's life, it is generally an energy of openness. If I am doing a reading for a client and they are at a crossroads I will not be able to read what the best path for them is, because the universe wants them to make a decision. I see it in my mind as a person surrounded by unlimited possibilities and potential; at a crossroads the seeker must decide what they want, and walk that path. Generally, the person I am reading for will be a little sad that the universe isn't telling them what they should do, and I like to remind them that the crossroads is a very powerful place where they get to decide!

Just as the crossroads is a decision point for the seeker whom the crossroads has presented itself to, it is that for the magician that wants to change their path. By invoking a crossroads, the magician is making a place of ultimate potential and shifting their reality! Given that the spirits also reside at the crossroads it is a supremely magickal place, and so doing powerful magick there is a given. I would like to point out that visiting an actual crossroads between the hours of midnight and three in order to do ones' magick is also super powerful. Besides being a magickal place I think there is an association in one's mind with meeting the unknown in the dark of night alone, that kind of bravery gives an added boost to any magick you may be doing.

Exercise in Magick

Making enchanted jewelry is a fun and easy way to begin to acclimate yourself to magick. If you've ever made your own jewelry this will be a fun exercise for you. If you've never made jewelry and don't have any access to making jewelry, you can enchant a piece of jewelry that you already own. Begin by deciding what kind of magick you would like to do; attract a lover, gain wisdom or success, or maybe you want to embrace your own power and self-confidence. Once you have decided what magick you are going to cast, you want to look at some reference books for color, and gem associations. For example, if I wanted to increase my courage, I might choose some tiger's eye stones to mix with carnelian. If I am making a necklace I might choose a pendant that has a symbol of strength and courage. You'll also want to pick up some herbs and oils that represent courage as well. Once you've got all your supplies you're ready to begin.

1.   Make your jewelry; I enjoy making necklaces and bracelets but you can make earrings or even rings if you are able. Pick out the stones and beads for their color correspondences that represent what you want to enchant your jewelry with.

2.   Once your jewelry is made you'll begin to create an incense mixture with the herbs and oils that you've picked out. I generally stick to three or five herbs, but you can choose however many feels right to you.

3.   Mix the herbs together with a mortar and pestle until you get a good scent. You use your intuition to know when you're done. If you can't tell, don't worry, just keep mixing.

4.   Once you've got your herb mixture all set, pick out one oil that you want to mix in with the herbs. You may find that you want to start over, and that is ok. It is normal in the beginning to feel you want to start over because, "it just isn't right."

5.   Take the oil and anoint your jewelry with it. Hold it in your hands and envision yourself achieving the goal that you are casting for. Once you've got a real strong vision in your mind blow that energy into the jewelry.

6.   Put the herb mixture in a little baggie, and then place your jewelry in the mixture. You can blow in the baggie again if you'd like with the vision of your success.

7.   Let the jewelry soak up the magick overnight. In the morning take out your jewelry and put it on. How beautiful that is!

8. Don't think about your spell anymore. The magick is set in motion, your thoughts will only lessen its success.

9. You can also keep your incense and put the jewelry in the baggie every night to recharge, but that is not necessary. Burn the incense, or bury it in the earth, when you're done with it.

10. Congratulations! You've successfully practiced magick!

When you give intent to an object you empower it. Utilizing oils and herbs that have been known to resonate with the desired outcome, so that vibration is informing the jewelry, as well as your energy body, when you wear it. This is a simple form of folk magick that is so very powerful and transformative. To decide a direction for your life, and then take action to create it is not only good magick, but it's good living. These tenets work in the mundane (non-magickal) world as well. To change your mind is to shift your world.

Shamanic Magick

Each tradition has its own unique flare, and I find shamanic magick to be very earthy. I can pick up a rock, blow my intention into it, and set that rock back down; magick. Feathers have inherent meaning. They resonate with the power of the birds; they connect the practitioner with the mysteries of the archetype as well as the beings. Feathers will show up almost as a portal, like the birds are saying, "talk to us". Incorporating rocks, feathers, and bones into your magickal practice is very shamanic, though I might argue these truths resonate through all the magickal practices.

I compared the shaman, the witch, and the sorcerer in the second chapter, and it seems as if I am trying to compare those definitions again.

Really, the only reason I consider this type of magick 'shamanic magick' is because it is a part of the Q'ero tradition that I have learned, and when I work with other witches they view it as more shamanic. That being said, there really isn't a big difference, they are just different tools to accomplish the same goals.

Since I gave you a magick exercise, here's a shamanic magick exercise, and you can define the difference for yourself.

Exercise in Shamanic Magick:

When you're trying to work through an issue, and you're having difficulty processing what to do, you can work with a stone.

1. Go outside, thinking about your issue, look for a palm sized stone. The first one that stands out to you is 'the one'. You can't do this wrong, so don't worry too much about it. Just pick up a stone.

2. Think about your issue, and everything that is involved. Now blow it all into that stone.

Ok, let's go over it again: pick up a stone, take a deep breath in, feel all the problems that are occupying your mind, and then blow it all into the stone.

3. When you're done you can just put the stone back on the earth and walk away. The earth is readily available and quite capable of transmuting your heavy energy, your bad thoughts, your sadness, and troubles into new life! The earth has the magnificent ability of taking heavy energy deep into the dirt and recycling it to create fertilizer for new growth. Metaphysical composting at its core!

Alternative 3. Take that stone home with you. Put it on your nightstand, or under your bed. You will definitely have dreams about the issue. When you wake up, write down your dreams. Take your stone with you wherever you go, in your pocket, in your purse, or however you'd like to keep it close. Hold on to it until your issue is resolved.

4. When the issue resolves you can either follow the instructions in step 3, leaving the stone on the earth and walking away. Or, you can decide that the issue was so significant that this stone is now a power object, holding the energy of your transformation, and integrate it into your altar.

Blowing into a stone is one of the easiest, and practical magickal practices for your day to day routine. No one will ever really notice what you are doing, or give you strange looks in your cubicle. Well they might, but then you just respond, "It's my lucky stone." Simple. The reason this is simple is because it works on a couple of different levels: first, it requires you to acknowledge your issue, bringing those thoughts to the surface. Many times we are in constant internal chatter, never really realizing all our brain energy is going towards things that bother us! By recognizing your thoughts and acknowledging them you are taking a moment to be in the 'Now'. Secondly, when you feel the energy of the thought and blow it out of you, it is a metaphorical purge, using the life breath with magickal intention to expunge your heaviness from you.

If you who want to go deeper into this exercise I would challenge you to find a stone that represents you, a stone that you identify with. Now go find a black river rock, and make sure it is bigger than the stone that represents you. Place the river rock below the stone of you and imagine your heavy energy constantly being absorbed into the black stone. When you have bad thoughts blow them into the black stone.

When you've got all the bad thoughts out of your head, try to have some gratitude thoughts, and then blow them into the stone of you. This little practice will constantly remind you to cleanse and recharge yourself; out with the heavy, in with the light.

Magick as Essence

Magick are essence teachings; understanding the essence of a thing grants you access to shape-shifting your own aura into that thing, thereby attracting that energy into your life. Your life changes because the resonance of your energy changes. It is like music. It is music.

When I was in high school I had to make a poetry book for my English class. I titled mine 'Essence' and proceeded to include various poems that I believed captured the essence of things. Looking back, the poems are obviously high school poems, but the concept of essence remains true to my core. The essence of a thing is its core, is its resonance, is the taste/sound/smell of a thing. To know the essence of a thing is to know it intimately. To know a thing intimately is to really allow it to permeate your core. To permeate your core is to become part of a thing. This is magick.

Magick is also simply a shift in consciousness, at will. To change your mind is to change your environment, literally. I had a revelation as I was ruminating on the concept of magick, and consciousness; my Sociology background had already trained me to step outside of society. I had to change my consciousness regarding my socialization in order to fully understand the concepts, and further to postulate my own theories. It is with this ability to deviate from social norms that I was able to deviate from consensual reality. Consensual reality tends to teach humans that they have no power, and no ability to shift their reality. Carlos Castaneda (1971), in his writings about

Don Juan Matus, spoke of shifting out of consensual reality in order to fully embrace power. These things are true.

You must not collude with consensual reality, you must realize that reality is malleable, and if you can train your mind to deviate from normal standards of experience, then you shift your experience. Allow the essence of things to integrate with your essence so that you can embody them, and shift yourself. This is the way of magick.

6

Training Your Thoughts & Words

When I was young, my mom taught me that there are two ways that a person can be in life: an optimist or a pessimist; she said you have the choice at every moment which to be. I had been very pessimistic when I was young. Once I decided that I would consciously look at life in an optimistic manner, and that it was a choice, things began working in my favor. Now, this is a lifetime practice. I still have moments of getting very down on myself, and the state of things. In these instances, I also watch how many aspects of my life resonate at the same frequency.

In magick I find the same to be true, that at every moment you must choose to be an optimist, with whatever your situation. Magick works on belief, and optimism is a state of mind. Many times people are not aware of the words they are using, of the dis-empowering stance they take in their language, or the reality that words are spells. Words are the verbal expression of thoughts. People are also not aware that they let their thoughts rule their minds, and if their words are disempowered, chances are their thoughts are as well. Your words are powerful, and you should watch what you say, and how you say it. Be aware of the web you are spinning, because, like a spider, it is sure that you will be living right in the middle of it.

My first lesson in training my thoughts and words came from a customer I had while working as a waitress. He was a regular customer, and we had grown close as I watched him read the entire bible, and then the Tao Te Ching; we would have philosophical religious conversations. A bit of a trickster himself, our conversations were never dull. One day I was showing him my art portfolio, and he was looking deeply into the meaning of each painting. Looking at one of my pieces I confided in him that, "I don't like how obsessive I can be, I wish I could stop being obsessive."

"Why do you call it obsessive?" he responded, "Every word has meaning, and the meaning that you are trying to convey could just as easily be called extremely focused."

With that one sentence he transformed my understanding of self from a fault to a strength. It blew my mind. I vowed from then on to begin paying attention to the words I used to define myself, and whenever I came across something as detrimental I would look for the good aspects of it.

Training your thoughts and words can be difficult in a society that values a busy mind. Sometimes our minds can be so full of words, and so quick to judge that it takes lots of practice to consciously slow them down. I have found that by training your words, you can sort of accidentally train your thoughts. As you stop yourself from saying words you become consciously aware of the thoughts that those words were coming from. Voila!! You have successfully begun to change your thoughts.

There are many reasons that you must train your thoughts and words, but some of the more important reasons are: 1. you can't receive psychic input if your mind is full of words. 2. If you are unaware of your thoughts then when thoughts that are not yours enter your head, you have a tendency to think they are yours. 3. As you gain magickal power your thoughts begin to manifest rather quickly. 4. Your words are magick, and weaving a web of un-empowered personal story will keep you un-empowered.

A quick disclaimer: I am in no way suggesting that people who experience trauma in life are responsible for their own trauma because their thoughts conjured it. Trauma happens. A person who experiences a traumatic experience shouldn't be blamed for their reality. At the same time, it is of benefit to not let trauma become the major life theme of one's story. Even if it happens over and over again, it is best to stop telling the story. (Unless that

Look at what you think of often, and begin to train yourself out of pessimism, jealousy, + rage. Learn that thoughts manifest, and dictate your REALITY

WHEN YOU CAN REMOVE YOURSELF FROM YOUR THOUGHTS THE MIND CAN BE FILLED WITH COMMUNICATION FROM THE GODS

They manifest into reality and are also accessible psychically.

WHEN YOU HAVE ATTAINED ENOUGH MANA YOUR THOUGHTS WILL MANIFEST QUICKLY.

Train

★

IF YOU DON'T LIKE YOUR THOUGHTS BUT ARE UNABLE TO STOP THEM THEN YOU MUST SPEND TIME WITH THEM TO FIND OUT **WHAT** IS THE ROOT OF THEIR REPETITION.

Be kind to yourself in your thoughts

IT IS A LIFETIME ENDEAVOR TO TRAIN YOUR MIND, BUT I HAVE FOUND IT IS HELPFUL IN TAKING RESPONSIBILITY FOR YOURSELF.

Your

Thoughts

IF SOMEONE IS DOMINATING YOUR THOUGHTS TAKE MEASURES TO DISCONNECT THEM FROM YOUR ENERGY FIELD, AND BE HONEST WITH YOURSELF ABOUT YOUR FEELINGS TOWARDS THEM.

story is being utilized to encourage social change). By making the trauma story a platform for change it is now a source of power.

You must train your thoughts so that they don't take you over. If your mind is full of words, then you are deaf to the words of spirit. Clearing your mind allows you to become more sensitive to psychic input. Now, from what I've experienced this isn't always true. Sometimes the spirits will yell! That is not the norm, however, and developing your relationship with spirit requires that you learn to clear your mind so that you may receive messages.

When I was first learning about magick, and psychic phenomena, I wanted desperately to be psychic (or some semblance of psychic-ness that I believed I hadn't attained yet). I also held a high regard for constant thoughts. In my belief I needed to be constantly thinking in order to be smart. I thought my mind chatter was telling of my intelligence. I was at odds with myself: I wanted more psychic input, and also I wanted to augment my mental prowess with constant thinking. I have come to realize that intelligence is often helped by spirits' guidance!

When I realized that I needed to start clearing out my clutter I felt it was an impossibility for me. I would think ad nauseam! One technique that I accidentally found helps is giving your thoughts a focal point, and a task. What am I feeling right now? Why? This tricky little ditty will connect your mind to your heart. Thinking (mind) about feeling (heart). By connecting your heart and your mind you will begin to feel more and more, until feeling is as important as thinking, and takes up as much space. In my experience feelings are the basis of psychic ability. When you have cleared your mind enough to be able to receive pictures you must also feel them to understand what is being shown.

Always work with your reality, and not against it, meaning don't beat yourself up over things that look impossible. Find ways to integrate them into possibility. Find the 'obsessive' and define it as 'extremely focused' within yourself. The same is true for your magick. Work with yourself when casting magick, and be creative with your direction. There are many ways to do magick, not just by the book.

Training your thoughts also helps to ensure that your mind is not being held captive by another. Now, it doesn't need to be a bad witch throwing curses your way and controlling your mind; it can be an energetically strong friend who really wants an ice cream, and now you are fantasizing about the varied flavors of frozen delight. Training your thoughts ensures that you know which thoughts are yours and which thoughts are coming from outside influences. Keep in mind that as you progress magickally, you become more sensitive, so you must take your own thought control training seriously.

I remember a time when I was in the midst of an enhancement in sensitivity; I was shopping and suddenly I was hit with an overwhelming sadness. I doubled over clutching myself and the tears bursting beyond my control. I thought, "That was weird!" and continued shopping. (It is a common occurrence during spiritual evolution to need to process through emotions that have built up over a lifetime). I turned down another aisle in the store, when out of nowhere I felt in love! In love! I felt intensely in love! I stopped, and looked around. These were obviously not my feelings, and I needed to acknowledge they were not mine. I realized that I was picking up on other peoples' vibes, and looked around to see who it could be. No one stood out, but I knew the feelings were not mine. That is the key! Know when the feelings are yours, and clear out emotions that are not yours. Do not lay claim to emotions, or thoughts, that are coming from somewhere else.

In magick it is very important to train your thoughts, as the more power you gain the more power your thoughts have. If you lay claim to thoughts and feelings that are not yours, you hand them your power. If your thoughts are often sad, angry, mean, or otherwise diminishing, you will create a world that mirrors that. Early on in my magickal pursuits I experienced people saying the most hurtful words to me about my beliefs. It was common, a theme that emerged: I was someone who could be diminished. As I gained more control over my thoughts my perspective changed, and I no longer was faced with such insulting opposition. It was a bizarre shift, but one that I noticed blatantly. I now keep a sort of internal tally of my words and focus; am I focusing on what is going wrong? How are people responding?

The words we choose to use are our story. When I began internalizing, and telling, the story of my ability to become extremely focused, I was able to utilize that energy and focus it on projects, and manifesting ideas. I took something that I thought was bad, and turned it in to a secret super power. My story began to change, and I saw my capabilities as being useful. In shamanic traditions one's traumas can be transformed into the source of their power. Once a memory is reclaimed, and transformed, it holds the ability to push you into extraordinary power.

Now see the magnificent beauty in the spinning of words. Words have inherent meaning. Every time you say a word be taken up into the smoke of its ether. Think in lavish and extravagant words and phrases, bending and twisting you into a conjurous dance. Nothing feels more alive and free than the creation of a rhythmic sentence. In your magick be sure to include chants that you create yourself, and write poems to your spirits. Let the power of words become fully realized in your consciousness. You are the spider; weave your web.

Exercise in Words

Over the next week I want you to be an observer of your conversations. Pay attention to what position you have in the story you are telling. At the end of the week I want you to write down:

1. The general themes you rely on
2. How you frame yourself in your stories
3. How people respond to you

Now, I want you to consciously change your language for one week. If you're not sure how to change your stories, then you must abstain from speaking the words that diminish you, or make you feel small. Sometimes just not speaking the words creates the shift. At the end of that week I want you to reflect on how you feel. Did shifting your language change your feelings?

Thoughts become words, and the other way around. It is impossible to speak of one without the other. When you gain power, your thoughts will begin to manifest more quickly, and your words will create your world. To attain power without having worked on training your mind is a sure way to self-destruct. At this point I need to reiterate: magick is not for everyone. If you don't want to bother with personal evolution, and self-awareness, then disengage from this path.

Power

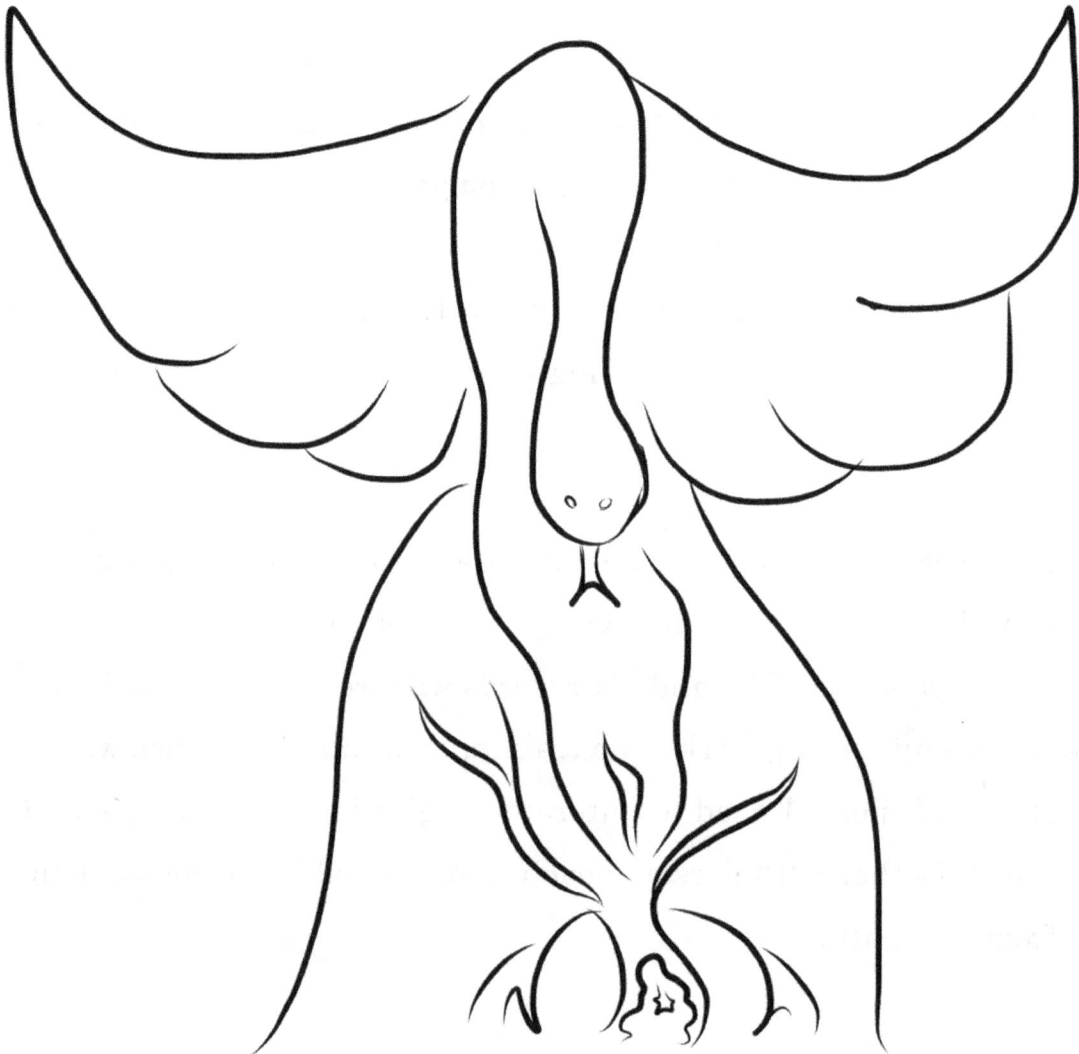

Power is a necessary subject when speaking of magick. One who practices magick but has no power, will not affect change. I have come into contact with people who have a negative association with the word 'power' and so have begrudgingly allowed my conversation, but held to their belief that power is bad. Power is neither good nor bad, it just is. I imagine it as strong energy, as the collusion of the cosmos within one's being. Power increases as mana is acquired. I am using the term mana as it is a concise anthropological and sociological term defined as, "Mana is a prime ingredient in magic(k). To those who believe in it, there exists in the world, everywhere, and in everything, an elemental force, a primary energy - mana." (Johnstone, 2007).

Firstly, to disown power is very much a part of the Christian paradigm of belief. It is generally from Christian practitioners that I have heard, "I have no power but for God". Karl Marx would argue, as would I, that convincing people to willingly give up their power, in the name of God, is a powerful tool of social control. Marxist social theory aside, I also find it humorous to hear people tell me they give up their power in a way that tells me they had never acquired power to give up in the first place. It is very easy to say you will relinquish power when you have none. In order to give up power you have to have tasted its delights. Giving up power once you've attained it is a very difficult feat. But let's discuss attaining power before we speak of giving it up.

Embracing power has many components, and the first one is accepting your own truth as part of reality. Claim the conviction of your arguments, beliefs, and perceptions, and have the courage to explore them. You must learn to stand up for yourself and argue with somebody without rolling over because you are afraid to trust your truth. Have you ever had an argument

Check That your actions Match your Words

IF YOU FIND THAT YOUR WORDS, AND ACTIONS DON'T MATCH UP, THEN YOU MUST STOP TALKING WHILE YOU GET REACQUAINTED WITH YOURSELF.

Do NOT TRUST SOMEONE'S WORDS IF THEY DO NOT MATCH THEIR ACTIONS, BUT BE AWARE THAT MANY TIMES PEOPLE ARE JUST UNAWARE OF THEIR INCONGRUENCE.

it is important that you seek out self awareness in order to keep your magick from devouring you.

make sure you are not lying to yourself

FURTHER, IF YOU FIND THEY ARE NOT MATCHING UP, YOU MUST **DILIGENTLY** SEEK OUT WHY.

YOUR INNER SELF MUST KNOW YOUR OUTER SELF.

with someone where they fought for their perspective with a fervor that forced you to bow down? That is power. Often in those situations, what is actually happening is an abuse of power. True power stands without needing to diminish the truth of others. But this example serves as a litmus test: when you step into power, people who used to overpower you in arguments are no longer able to. If you identify more with the person who uses power to win arguments, I want you to acknowledge that. Know that you were trained through upbringing to survive through use of great power, but in order to progress in the magickal path, you must learn how to allow others to stand in their power. Practicing magick means that you will continuously be self-reflective, and evolving. Stagnation does not exist on this path.

Becoming a magickal practitioner requires you to claim power. When you start to claim power your energy field becomes larger, more intense, and will manifest your weaknesses on your physical body. As a magickal practitioner you must, in your journey to claim power, also continue to work on integrating your shadow and moving past your desires to invoke trauma into your life. If you are sourcing your actions from pain, hurt, or anger, then you are letting your shadow drive. In order to integrate your shadow, you need to acknowledge it, and look to the root of your feelings. Once you accept the roots, then you can grow. The stronger your power, the more intense your traumas and shadows. To claim power without ever desiring to heal yourself (or others) you will begin to manifest sickness. This is the danger of the magickal path; realize the implications as you embark on the journey. With great power, comes great responsibility (to yourself and others). Sometimes magickal practitioners are unaware, or ignore, this caveat and will self-destruct from their own power.

Power is intensified energy. When you can pray to the universe, and know you are heard, then you are in power. Many people think they are in power, and cling to false hope of being heard; this is different. When you speak to god/desses and hear immediate response, you are in power. Also, a good way to measure if you are actually in power is: when people try to dismiss your practice as being fake, you are not threatened; you know your experience and your power in a very tangible way. The authenticity of knowing is beautiful to behold.

I have on occasion been asked what my best story of magick is from people whose lust for power shines through their eyes, and resounds in the stories that they say they've heard following my response. "I've heard of a man with a magick stick who could bend it, and in the bending, bed any woman he wanted," I was told once.

"Riiiiiight..." I think sarcastically to myself, interesting that this is what you value in magick: control. If this sounds familiar to you, and you think that it sounds like a great idea to try to control people, I want you to skip ahead to my section on bad magick. Consent is a very important idea. You are not to do magick on people, or for people, without their consent. There are a few caveats: you can do magick on the energy between you and another person, or you can do magick for a person if it will benefit them.

These two cases, however, are not straight forward. Sometimes when you know a person needs healing magick, and you tap in to work on them, you will feel the spirits saying, "No. No, you are not to interfere. We are doing work here. There is a lesson to be learned."

In this scenario, you must not exert your power to try to intervene, else you are stunting that person's personal evolution. You cannot always run in as a savior; that is not the purpose of this path. You must always be in communion with the spirits that you work with, be that God, god/desses,

you need to attain power in order to create change.

POWER

PART OF ATTAINING POWER IS TO FACE YOUR FEARS WITH

courage

TRICKERY

MANY TIMES POWER REQUIRES YOU TO LAUGH AT YOURSELF.

Power is complicated. You don't want to be taken over by lust for power, but you need to gain power to get into flow with a higher vibration of power.

You need to heal your energy field in order to carry power. A fragmented energy body will cause much pain.

angels, spirit guides, ancestors, or whoever you work with. Pay attention to their nuances, because often there is a much larger picture happening, and you must not interfere.

Another form of magick that is in the grey area is working on the energy between you and another person. We will often come upon situations where we have tension with someone, and your first idea may be to cast against them. Don't. Trust me. The way to work with this scenario is to acknowledge your role in the tension, and then work your magick on the energy between the two of you. The Peruvians would call this a hucha mijuy, or eating of heavy energy. You can use your magick to process the energy between the two of you, as long as you have both parties' highest good at heart.

In a relationship, any relationship, there is you, the other person, and the energy between you. This energy becomes its own being, with needs, and desires. Working magick on the tension between two people is to work magick on this being, the being of your relationship. You work with it, and treat it like you would a spirit. Find out how it can resolve its tension and do magick for that.

As a cautionary tale, I would highly urge anyone wishing to begin a journey on the magical path to become self-reflective before you ever even cast a spell. You must understand who you are, what your motivations are, and where they come from before you cast magick. Lack of this self-awareness will cause many negative effects on you. You have been warned. Personal responsibility is your mantra, and you will be responsible for how you wield your power.

A funny side note about power: when your energy field has evolved to a certain level, you will begin to notice that other people are affected by your presence. I find this funny, because it seems to be the spirits working through energetic vibration. I have noticed that *empowered* individuals will affect the experiences and energy of the people they come into contact with. I don't consider this a form of imposing your will on another, but rather the hilarity of energy interacting and intertwining. The spirits are always pushing us towards personal revolution.

I was once told a story about power by a shaman in Peru. He said the curandero and the brujo are on the same path, they both must attain power. At a certain point the accumulation of power has reached its climax. The brujo continues after power for power's sake, whereas the curandero gives up their power and pursues healing. Now, I'm not sure how I feel about the labels that are being used, but I do appreciate the moral of the story. It is an explanation of how to progress in the magickal path, and how to approach power. It is also a bit confusing, right? How does one continue healing people if they've given up their power? I will come back to this question.

Power is a lifelong process; most realities within magick are. I am of the belief that at any moment I could make the choice to continue after power because it is seductive. At every moment I make a choice to pursue compassion. It is a struggle for me. There are many moments where slight indiscretions against me are met with the thought, "How dare you do that to ME!! Do you know who I am?!" This is the lust of power speaking. This is ego. If these sorts of thoughts are not put in check when they arise, or looked into deeper and their roots and processed, the possibility of their dominion over your energy body is a very real.

Power is seductive. Once you have attained it, you will have difficulty giving it up. You may find that the struggle ebbs and flows, so sometimes you are not even aware of it, and other times you are in an all-out battle not to hurt someone with your mind.

WHAT DO YOU **FEEL?**

Who MAKES YOU TIRED?

Who gets tired around you?

ARE THOSE YOUR feelings?

You makes you feel Happy!

at ease

alive

mad

IRRITABLE

SAD

peaceful

BE AWARE OF YOUR

LEARN TO BE EMOTIONALLY SELF SUSTAINED

Hyper

Build Boundaries So That You don't get fed on

Recognize when you are feeding on someone else.

Powerful

ENERGY

and whose energy you permit in your field.

Remember, true power stands side by side with others, it does not dominate, it stands in its own truth and allows for other truths to coexist.

Giving up power once you had attained it is an interesting aspect of magick. I told you what the shaman said about gaining power for powers' sake, or giving up power in order to heal people. From what I've seen and experienced when enough mana is acquired, and a large amount of power is attained, it is at that point that one relinquishes the quest for power and puts their efforts into being *in flow* with power in order to accomplish their work. In other words, I agree with the shaman, but I don't think you are supposed to give up power; how else would you heal people? You must give up the reins of power, and instead be one with power. You must attain power in order to have a large enough energy body to hold the energy of power, it is at that point that you no longer have to attain more. Once you are a strong enough you can ride the waves.

It is a natural evolution of the magickal practitioners path to have their focus redirected once they have gone through the trials to gain power. A terrible amount of energy needs to be put forth in order to gain insights into one's reality, their true essence, and their shadow. I remember spending an inordinate amount of time gathering this information about myself, and about life, or archetypal truths. Then there was a point, not a point I remember, but a turning point where my efforts were less concerned with 'leveling up' and more with practical application. It was a subtle change. The epitome of that shift in reality was that I found myself asking, "Why?" much less often. I stood in the power of my own knowing.

8

Ancestors

During a family gathering, when I was 13, there was an incident. Tension had built within the family because my uncle had sent out letters to his siblings informing them that Santa was a lie, and an un-Christian thing to tell your children. My mom was furious. The idea that all the kids in the family, that still believed, were going to be told, was maddening. It was a battle of mythology. This tension culminated at Christmas. Everyone was sitting down for dinner when I saw my mom come into the house from the backyard. As if a flash of lightning, my uncle followed her in a fervor, standing in the door he yelled, "Witch! She's a witch! She's a witch!"

I stood up wanting to protect my mother. I stood up with all the rage in the world, and immediately crumbled into tears. My Nana took me into the other room while the aunts restrained my uncle against the wall. He kept yelling. I couldn't stop my sobs. I didn't understand my tears. I wanted to protect my mother, but this seemed like an emotional response to much more. Not until years later did I understand. My sister turned 30, and the family gathered to celebrate her milestone. Now, I'm not sure if I have mentioned this yet, but I'm Italian. My family is large, and we like to gather and celebrate. My sister's birthday was wonderful, and I felt at peace with the whole family; a peace that I have struggled to attain through my own lessons, and journey.

Later that night, as I sat with my thoughts, I thought about my uncle, and how kind he had been to me at the party. He seemed completely accepting, though I live everything that he fears, or admonishes. I slipped into my thought, and as I did, a past life memory jolted in my mind. "She's a witch!" resonated through me.

Always

MY SPIRITS TEND TO LIKE WINE AND TOBACCO.

REMEMBER TO FEED THE

TO FEED AND BE FED IS TO BE IN A CONSTANT STATE OF PRAYER AND COMMUNION.

Spirits

TO BE IN CONSTANT CONTACT WITH THE SPIRITS YOU SHOULD GET INTO A RHYTHM OF GIVE & RECEIVE.

TO FIND OUT WHAT THEY DESIRE TALK TO THEM. TRUST YOUR INTUITION. IF YOU ARE NOT SURE, MAKE AN OFFERING, THEN CONCENTRATE ON YOUR FEELINGS. IT IS A MIRROR.

I realized why his screams, so many years ago, had affected me. Well, besides being a shitty thing to do at a family gathering, there was more to his words. It was a memory of my past. A memory of the murder of witches. All witches are my ancestors, as well as my actual familial ancestors.

Ancestors are the most important part of magick, and living magickally. Shamanic societies have known this for as long as history has existed. I only recently realized this. When I first began my studies into magick, I had taken an Anthropology of Witchcraft course. In this course I learned of ancestor worship, and the importance of giving sacrifice, and reverence, to the ancestors. Often this was accompanied with the idea that if you didn't appease the ancestors, then they would wreak havoc on your life. I didn't like the idea of having dead family judge me, so I all but dismissed ancestor work. I would pay it lip service, and visit the Dia De Los Muertos celebrations, without fully embodying any understanding. Ancestor work took a back burner to my magickal repertoire. It wasn't until my Nana passed that I began to truly, physically embody, an understanding. I say physically embody because if I don't feel something in my body, if I don't have a feeling that resonates through my body with a concept, then I don't truly get it.

My Nana was very close to me. I can't explain it in normal terms, we didn't chat and gossip together, we actually probably didn't really even speak all that much. I just felt close to my Nana, and I could tell that she felt close to me. I actually stood up to my Nana in very public ways, on numerous occasions, that I would have assumed would make her dislike me. We had a bond. When she passed that bond grew, and thickened, into supple roots connecting me to my family tree. Suddenly, from the other side, she was my bridge to our magickal heritage, and social graces are unimportant compared to the truth. She now tells me her version of the stories I had heard growing up. She shows me her truth, her motivations, and her connection to me.

Before she passed, I was able to ask her about our family connect to 'the old religion'. I had read Raven Grimassi's works, and discovered that Italian lineages have a tradition of the aunts and grandmothers passing on the old knowledge to the grandchildren who show promise (Grimassi, 2003). I had the sense of wonder as I thought to ask my Nana if she had been taken aside by the aunts. At the next family gathering I took a seat next to her in the kitchen, and asked her if the aunts had ever taken her aside. She laughed, "Yes. Yes, I was taken aside by the crazy aunts, and I laughed at them."

"What!?" I exclaimed, appalled at the idea that she hadn't taken them seriously.

"Yeah, I laughed at them and made fun of them, and they said I would never learn so they stopped teaching me."

I was aghast. My Nana was the thirteenth child, and she had often joked with me that she used to have a mole on her cheek, just like mine. But it got too big, so she had it removed. The mole on my cheek was a connection to her. My Nana had laughed at the aunts, and so they stopped teaching her. My direct lineage was lost. In the years before my Nana's passing, her Nana, or who I refer to as Nona, made herself present to me, and I had been learning our lineage through her. Now that my Nana is on the other side, I connect with her, and Nona has stopped coming through.

It is funny to me how many memories of Nana take a magickal turn now. I remember a big family trip to Las Vegas, where we all took the train. Most of that trip is a blur, except for one snippet. My Nana like the National Enquirer, and she had a copy with her. On one of the pages there was a big blue dot, which was being claimed as a magical dot. I was playing the claw machine, trying to get a stuffed animal that I'm sure I had no need of. My

Nana showed me the dot, and told me to rub it before I played again. It seemed fun, so I rubbed that blue dot, and then put a quarter in the claw machine. As my Nana watched, I secured a stuffed toy with the claw, and to my amazement, the claw held, and I actually won it!

At the time I was so excited, and jumping around. That blue dot was magic, I thought. I asked to rub it again, and then I played again, but this time it didn't work. It didn't matter though, because my Nana was witness to when it had worked, and we shared that moment of mystery together. Now when I think of that memory, I see it through her eyes. She didn't think the dot was magick, she thought I was. She wanted to see what my belief could do, and before I had *thought* about it, I was able to manifest that claw machine's winnings. Little memories like this flood in occasionally, and now I realize that our whole relationship was based on magick.

When it comes to ancestry, many people speak of visiting the land of their ancestors. As is the theme of my journey, I understood the theory of it, but didn't really pay it much mind. I could philosophically understand that the land of ones ancestors is full of its connection to their past, but until I could visit Italy it was all theory. I had been to Holland, and half of my origins are Danish and Dutch, but there was no real resonance there. It was beautiful, just like every other foreign place I had visited, but it didn't feel like home.

I've always identified as Italian, and the amount of pride I've felt for that identity is probably due to the fact that I *look* Italian. I'd always wanted to visit the soil of my people; to go to my origin, and connect with the echoes. I told the universe that I wanted to go to Italy, but that if I did, I needed to go with a magick woman, and learn the magick of the land. Remember the story I told you in chapter 5?

On the plane to Italy, for my first time, I could feel the magick of the trip affecting me. I would suddenly be overwhelmed with emotion, breathing slowly. I decided not to watch the inflight movie, but to instead focus on the feelings. I had also become aware of a desire to find a sameness between myself and the Italian stewardesses. "I have her hair type. Isn't it interesting how she styles it" or "look at her fingers, they are thick like mine." These thoughts were looking for a commonality: body types, postures, beauty. It was as if looking at these women could prepare me to return home, the land of magick that runs through me.

I was in awe of how magick had gotten me there. On a plane because I won a travel prize, because I had tarantulas on my head, and now I am headed to Italy to learn the Tarantella from an Italian Shaman, Alessandra Belloni. The Tarantella a traditional song and dance that would cure women from the mythical bite of the spider. The energy of tarantula was with me, initiating me into her mysteries, and teaching me the mysteries of woman's reproductive power. Blood mysteries in the land of my blood lineage. It was bursting with so much magick that my tears were spontaneous and often. I was overwhelmed with the beauty, connection, and the return home in such a magickal way.

Italy was everything I imagined, and more than I could have anticipated. I actually *felt* home. I could feel the blood of my lineage pulsing through me as I learned the drumming, dancing, and especially when my feet were on the soil. I imagined I would feel some connection, but I didn't realize I would finally have a revelation of belonging somewhere. The people all felt like family, and my body reflected the norm of this place. I hadn't understood how much I had internalized a 'differentness' growing up in America. Or just how much I felt I didn't belong just by how I looked. It seems strange, because I don't really look that much different than everyone else. But, I always felt like I didn't look like anyone else, and that there must be a place where I was the same. It's really difficult to write this because it doesn't sound very significant, but in Italy I was overwhelmed with feeling like I belonged, like I looked like I belonged.

If you have a chance to visit the land of your heritage, or ethnic lineage, I would strongly suggest it. Remember though, it's not guaranteed that you will feel a connection. I did not feel any connection in Holland. You may find you feel connection in places that you wouldn't anticipate, and I would urge you to take note; pay attention. These places are power centers for your spiritual ancestor connection. We have the ancestors of our family, and the ancestors of our spiritual journey. You are connected to both, and will have profound experiences with both.

To connect to one's ancestors is to begin to know the pattern of your birth, and the foundation of your reality. Families are different, though cultures have many similarities. These similarities bind us together and teach us of our passions. To connect to our ancestors is to allow the sorrow, the shame, the joy, and the beauty of all those who have come before us, and shared our name. It is a communion of eternity, as time has carried us through our family's evolution. We are but the next piece, and we are the ancestors of our future. Acknowledging and strengthening this connection builds a fierceness in one's self knowledge. We must always remember our ancestors and accept our place as the next step in their evolution.

Ancestor Activity

We all have ancestors, whether blood relatives, or relatives of the family you were raised in. The ancestors that may work with you the most intensely will be the ones you actually had a connection with on the physical plane. Both of my grandmothers passed away, but only my Nana makes contact regularly. It may be because I reach out to work with her more than any of my other ancestors; partly because she has opened the door to all my Italian ancestral knowledge, and partly because she liked me when she was alive. We had a connection, we always did. That relationship became palpable when she passed. My other grandmother loved me, but our connection wasn't as strong. Whenever I try to tap in to her, and say hi, she will give me the impression that she's busy with other work.

I was given a very strong message from spirit that ancestor work must be done every day. This connection starts with a daily dialogue, and will grow over time. We have the ancestors living within us, in our blood lines. We are only the ancestors of the future, and we must realize that we stand on the shoulders of those who have come before. They have lived here, in this earthly existence and have learned many things that we can gain knowledge from. It is in this that we must honor the stories of where we come from, and in a shamanic path we must also involve ourselves in healing our ancestral line, healing those stories through our own story.

1. Pick a family member that you've known and think about them while putting out the request for contact. If you do not have any family member to choose, then I want you to reach out to a spiritual ancestor.

1. Close your eyes, and think of your connection to your ancestor, or your spiritual family

2. Ask for your guides to connect you to this ancestor.

3. Start to talk to them (whether or not they have appeared in your mind's eye), create a dialogue to build a connection. You do not have to speak out loud. Thinking your conversation creates it.

4. Do this in the morning every day.

5. (Optional, but super fun) Build an ancestor altar. It can be the top of a shelf, or anywhere really. Include pictures of family, and the family that has passed on. Start to add items that connect you to them. This will be different for everyone, so it is completely up to you. Whenever you want to talk to your ancestors, burn a tea-light candle, and spend time with your altar.

Know that you are not alone, you are connected to the infinite knowledge of all of history. It has been said often that the spirits are there, waiting for us to start talking to them. When you start talking, you will never feel alone again. The spirits are all around, with different personalities and input. You will realize you were never alone, and that there is always something new to explore. Explore, knowing you are the continuation of everyone who came before you.

9

Dreams & Initiations

As a child I would have night terrors, a fact that was probably terrifying to my mom. I would often wake up screaming. I remember when I was around fifteen, vividly, dreaming that I had developed lesions, from the black plague, on my neck. I woke up terrified, running into my mom's room to show her. I was sure I was dying. It was only a dream. At least that's what I was told. That's what society tells us, but I am sure that I was having a past-life memory, or a human collective consciousness memory. I don't really care which idea you subscribe to, only that you acknowledge the importance of dreams.

The world of science has studied dreams, and there are hundreds of books on dream interpretation; dreams are a fascinating reality that happens when we are not awake. Or maybe we are more awake in the dreamtime. I used to believe that dreams were just a way for the brain to process the day's activities, which generally science has found. Now, I am more of the belief that there are many different versions of dreams. There are ethereal dreams, everyday minutia dreams, prophetic dreams, and metaphor dreams. Other shamanic practitioners, and witches, will tell you the importance of lucid dreaming; that one must have power over their dreamtime in order to fully claim power in the waking world. Don't let that be a daunting thought. Magick is a lifetime endeavor, and you will find that the world of magick is open to you even if you haven't learned, or mastered, everything there is to know.

As I mentioned there are many different types of dreams, because in my experiences this is what I have found. My favorite, and what I seem to experience the most, are metaphor dreams; the ones that help me to learn a lesson, and evolve. These are part of the reason that it is so important to keep a dream journal: knowing ones' own subconscious metaphors isn't necessarily a given. By keeping a dream journal, you are able to train yourself in your own metaphors. Usually six months to a year after the dream, when you look back at your journal, you will see what the dream was actually trying to tell you. Now you know a little more about yourself, and how your subconscious tries to communicate with you. Again, I keep a dream journal, but I don't necessarily write in it every day. Sometimes, I don't write down my dreams, and instead walk with them, letting their story permeate my waking life. Occasionally, I am awoken in the middle of the night because my dream requires I write it down if I would like to go back to sleep.

Ethereal dreams are the ones that are actually happening in the dreamtime; they are real, your actions are real, and you are actually communicating with spirits, or people. In ethereal dreams you can meet up with other people and work through things. Maybe you have further communication to have that is not being had in the mundane realm, or maybe your spirits meet in the ethereal to practice magickal acts, or maybe you have a past life together that you need to process through. These are all possibilities in the context of the ethereal dream, but what you really must understand is that ethereal dreams are really happening. Your spirit body is interacting with the spirit realm. This is where lucid dreaming occurs, as well. Occasionally I have met up with aggressors on the ethereal realm, they have attacked me, and I have woken up with bruises. Now, this doesn't happen often, and if you are careful in all of your relations, you will probably not have a magickal aggressor try to attack you.

Occasionally the etheric dreams and metaphor dreams will combine themselves, so that you are both being given metaphors, as well as interacting with actual spirits. Living in the dorms at UCSC, my studio apartment was located just on the outskirts of Merrill college. Situated spitting distance from the schools provost, I was both away from the general populous of 18 year olds, and tucked into the redwood forest. I had managed to get the dorm all to myself, and my sliding glass door opened to a balcony surrounded by dense, beautiful, redwoods. I was in the most magickal place I had ever been in; a secluded hermit, practicing witchcraft and cramming for finals. I also made time to paint, and found I am fond of procrastinating, which oddly led to taking up jogging around the school's track. The track, which felt haunted in the evenings, overlooked a beach view. It was in this magickal place that old Picasso tried to kill me.

I call him old Picasso because there are stages of Picasso's life, and they are distinctly different from one another. Old Picasso is a little bit terrifying, in the way he carries his truth, deadpan in the wells of his eyes. It was an ethereal dream, and felt more real, more full of color, and more like the repercussions of my dream decisions rested on my shoulders. I had a huge mountain to climb, which was a metaphor, but I noticed that to the left of the mountain was a small staircase that would lead me to the same peak. As I walked towards it I felt a shadow begin to mirror me. As I turned towards the stairs I saw old Picasso staring back at me from the top. His vehement presence warned of rape and murder as he warned me against the stairs, and pointed towards the mountain. I didn't understand why old Picasso had violence towards me, and I definitely did not want to struggle to climb that mountain when there was this small staircase. Old Picasso lunged at me, and my consciousness startled awake, the clouds of the dream still lingering, when I felt the spirit of a wolf enter my body. I became a wolf; my teeth felt the sensation of ripping flesh, a fatal wound if applied to the jugular. I knew how to kill a man. Wolf was my spirit; I am wolf.

I was waking from that dream when I saw a black shadow at the window of my apartment. I knew it was an apparition, but I wasn't prepared to deal with it. I turned my head and went back to sleep, but my dreams were back in my room, and the shadow figure was still there. I called out my magickal teacher's name. My consciousness flew left, away from the apparition, was drawn into the cauldron on my altar, and I was somewhere else. Later I reflected on that dream as a lesson in how to kill an attacker; I have large teeth, and they can be utilized. I now, however, believe that dream was an initiation. The wolf spirit entered me, and I became wolf. I was initiated into a new reality. Also, combining metaphor with etheric, I needed to do the work, instead of looking for shortcuts.

Each type of dream has a purpose, and once you familiarize yourself with their differences, you can begin to work with them. Everyday minutia dreams are the ones where you are a rat learning a maze. Your brain is reliving aspects of your daily life in order to learn it more quickly. This type of dream can be amazing for math equations, and other day-to-day problems that need solving. Your brain will decide on what needs to be worked through, unless you intend it before you go to sleep. This is quite simple: write out a problem that you would like to solve in your dreams, fold the paper and put it under your pillow. (You don't actually need to write it out, you can just think your intention, but many times writing it out helps). Then in your dreams you will likely solve the problem, or at least get past the blockages that were keeping you from solving the problem in waking reality. This can be very helpful in your studies.

Prophetic dreams are just what they sound like: when you dream an event that hasn't happened yet, and then it happens in your waking life. I sometimes have prophetic dreams, though not often. I also made a dream catcher with the intention of weaving my reality in the dreamtime, so that I can do magick while sleeping. I have often joked that I'm not sure if I'm magick or psychic, because there seems to be a thin line between creating a reality, and foreseeing a reality. I imagine the truth actually encompasses both, intertwined in a poetic nuance.

I find that prophetic dreams are nice to have because you get a 'heads up' for what's coming. But what use is a 'heads up' when you want to change something? My theory is that you have prophetic dreams so that you can decide whether or not you want that occurrence to actually happen. If you dream that something bad occurs, you can wake up and take actions that will stave off that reality, or prepare you. Sometimes you cannot avoid the prophecy. For example, let's say you have a dream of an interpersonal conflict with someone you care about. By knowing the type of argument you are going to have you can make preparations, like an endearing note, or take precautions, and make preparations to listen, not get offended, and find a way to communicate fully. Most likely you need to work with the spirit world to see why the event is going to occur, and see multiple sides of the story. Is there something important that needs to be taken away from it? A prophecy is still malleable, at least a little bit. The spirits gave you the information beforehand for a reason, so, find out what it was.

I mentioned a dream catcher. You thought I was just going to skim over that. Fear not, I will reveal many of my secrets. I am not trained in Northern Native American traditions, and my creation of a dreamcatcher could be considered cultural appropriation, except that I am utilizing the symbol, but for my own magickal intentions.

I am a weaver. The idea of having a spider web above my bed has amazing

YOUR GUIDES WILL VISIT YOU IN YOUR DREAMS

WRITE YOUR DREAMS IN A JOURNAL TO LEARN ABOUT YOUR SUBCONSCIOUS, AND ALSO TO KEEP TRACK OF WHAT THE SPIRITS ARE TRYING TO TELL YOU.

YOU MAY FIND YOUR DREAMS ARE PROPHETIC DIRECTLY OR THROUGH METAPHOR.

Dreams Are Significant and purposeful

THEY ARE THE KEY TO YOUR SUBCONSCIOUS

TRUST THEM they are Sacred

magickal possibilities. When I was a kid I would buy dreamcatchers and put them over my bed as a means of 'catching bad dreams', but that never really worked for me. Most likely because it was from a culture that I didn't actually practice, and mass produced for profit. My witchcraft works best when I make it myself. Now, as a witch, the idea of a web associated with dreams has many more possibilities. The spider is a weaver, and weaves their own reality through words, and energetic attachments. The spider resides in the middle of its web. This is also true for humans. We weave our realities through our words, and energetic attachments, and then live there. A witch is responsible for their own web. (Others are also responsible for their own webs, but without the cosmological understanding of this reality, we really can't blame them for their ignorance).

Everything in your life can be utilized as a metaphor, and that metaphor can be intended with magick. With the dreamcatcher, I made it myself and intended it to be a tool of manifestation. Now when I go to sleep I have given power to myself as a weaver in the dreamtime: weaving the energetic patterns of my reality in my dreams so that they will manifest in the waking world. Magick: it is whatever you intend it to be.

Lastly, when it comes to dreams and magickal initiations, I have found that your dreams will change once you've come into power. Now, it's not necessarily a simple concept to explain, but it is easily understood in its manifestation. When you start to be at one with the energy of the universe, claiming some of your own power, you will begin to 'win' in your dreams. What do I mean by that? I mean, if you have dreams where you are running, or being chased, or you can't unlock the door in time, these will all but disappear. You will begin to have dreams where you are the victor; you defeat the malice that attacks you. You are no longer running away.

Magickal initiations are many. I could probably write an entire book on that concept alone, and I'm sure others have. When you engage on the magickal path, you are opening the door to be initiated into the mysteries. As you evolve magickally, you are initiated into new realms, and new understandings. Sometimes you are initiated in the dreamtime, other times you are initiated during waking life, but you will definitely have significant dreaming while being initiated. Again, get a dream journal. It doesn't have to be fancy, and you don't have to write in it every day. Get rid of any of your preconceived rules about a dream journal that would lend to you not using one. They are for your own understanding, your own evolution. Dreams are very important, and you will be dreaming all of your life, so it is imperative that you make a relationship with the dreamtime. You can do that however you would like, it is your dreamtime, and your relationship.

Dream Exercise:

Dreaming can be very useful and functional for your everyday encounters. If you have something you are trying to work through in your life, I want you to try this dreaming exercise.

1. Write down the issue that is occurring and what you need help with

2. You can either fold the paper, and put it under your pillow, or you can create a dream altar, and put it on your altar.

   a. Dream altars are as different as each practitioner. My dream altar has a stone for flying, a stone for seeing, and a stone for delving deep, on it. That is it. Others may have deities, beads, jewelry, incense, or whatever they like. When you create a dream altar, make it near your bed, and decorate it with symbols that are important for you, and will help you in your dreaming.

b. Once the dream altar has been made, you want to energize it, or bring it to life. I find that a ceremony, or prayer, where you use an oil, an incense, and intention, works just fine. Once you've set the intent, now you have created a magickal tool to aid you on your journey.

c. Every night, before bed, spend some time with your altar. Clean it, or gaze at it; give it your attention. Your attention gives it life. If you let it stagnate with inattention, then it will stop working for you.

3. Your dreams will definitely be regarding the issue at hand. If you don't understand the dreams, or don't remember them, talk to your guides. Ask them for greater clarity, or for help in remembering. As you work this dream endeavor, it will begin to work for you. Write it all down, because I promise you will forget, and it is important to mark when magick occurs.

Working with your dreams is a fundamental aspect. The dreamtime is very important. The more you write them down, the more they will make sense, but also the more you will remember your dreams. By knowing that your dreams are important, you are empowering them, and yourself.

10

Power Objects

I have collected many power objects on my journey. Power objects are not static, they have life, and they transform. I have also found that these power objects will ebb and flow in response to my needs. So, something that was super powerful a couple of years ago, may not carry the same power now because it came into my life, served a purpose for me, and them transformed into something else. Sometimes power objects stop being powerful for you specifically because they need to be powerful for someone else. It is also true that an object will hold power longer if you continue to imbue it with your belief in its power, and continuous working. Power objects, like everything in magick, have a life of their own, and cannot be expected to stay the same forever.

I love working with power objects. I specifically utilize stones when performing a healing on clients. Each power object carries a specific frequency, and I utilize those frequencies to interrupt my client's frequency, and bring about change. a collection of power objects is like a medicine chest, a sacred bundle, or as the Q'ero call it, a Mesa. Mesa means table in Spanish, and in the Q'ero tradition, you bring your prayers to the table, and speak with the spirits. A collection of power objects translates to life experiences that brought power to an individual. Power objects can be many different things, and you will find on your journey that you encounter power objects, in their varied forms, specific to your path.

I have many power objects, but the ones I work with daily are stones. Each of my stones has a purpose, and an energetic frequency: lightning, death, vision. These stones come to me from places I have found them, whether Peru, Mount Baldy, Australia, Costa Rica, or at the park down the street. When I find them they have a story to tell me, many times about myself. The stones have been here since the beginning of time, and they hold the energy of all of that history; they are imbued with the energy of life, and also like to be moved, as movement comes quite difficult to them. Stones carry the energy of the beginning of time, of creation. To speak with rocks is to talk to the mysteries directly. And each stone generally has a story to tell, and a power to imbue.

As I have stated before, I am a practitioner of the Peruvian Q'ero tradition, and there are many books on the subject of their beliefs and practices. I started using stones in a specific way to their traditions, but even before that training I had utilized stones in my magickal practice. There are books upon books that can be used as reference for the meanings of stones. I have, and do, use stones in that way as well. Currently I am wearing Labradorite because the spirits told me to, and when I looked up its meaning it is said to aid in connecting intuition to intellect, as well as keeping the aura clear and strong. I also use stones irrespective of their metaphysical associations, like this rock that I found at a park that makes me feel like my soul is about to fly. I call this my flying stone, and though I am not sure what the actual name of the stone is, I have named it for its utility. So, there are many ways to work with stones, but these are some of the ways that I work with them.

When working on a client, I will use the utility of a stone for a specific purpose. If I need to shock someone into seeing clearly, I will put my lightening stone on the area that needs illumination. As I mentioned before, my stones are like a medicine chest, and each stone has a meaning, a utility. I will prescribe my death stone to release old patterns, to bring an end to energetic imprints that have past their time. I use a serpent stone to dive deep into the subconscious and find the roots of past traumas, to push past the boundaries of self-protection, and shed the skin of old stories.

COLLECT STONES FROM THE
PLACES OF POWER THAT EXPERIENCE.
YOU VISIT, AND FROM
PLACES WHERE YOU HAVE POWERFUL EXPERIENCE.

FAKE BONES CAN
CARRY THE POWER
OF REAL BONES
WITH
YOUR
INTENTION

SOME OBJECTS
ARE IMBUED
WITH POWER OF
THEIR OWN,
OTHERS ARE
MADE SACRED
BY A PRACTITIONER,
AND YET OTHERS
ARE A MIXTURE
OF BOTH.

WITH EVERY POWER
OBJECT THAT YOU
COLLECT OR MAKE
YOU INCREASE YOUR
ENERGY FIELD, BUT
ALSO YOU WILL
HAVE TO GO
THROUGH
A PERSONAL
EVOLUTION
IN ORDER TO
CARRY THAT
INCREASE.

POWER objects

SOMETIMES THEY WILL
DISAPPEAR, AND YOU
MUST LET THEM. THE
PRACTICE OF NON-ATTACHMENT
IS VERY IMPORTANT, ESPECIALLY
IN REGARDS TO POWER.

SOMETIMES
PETS WILL
CHOOSE YOU,
AND THEY
TOO WILL
ACT AS
POWER
OBJECTS.

YOU WILL
GAIN MORE
OBJECTS AS
YOU PROGRESS
OFTEN AS
GIFTS.

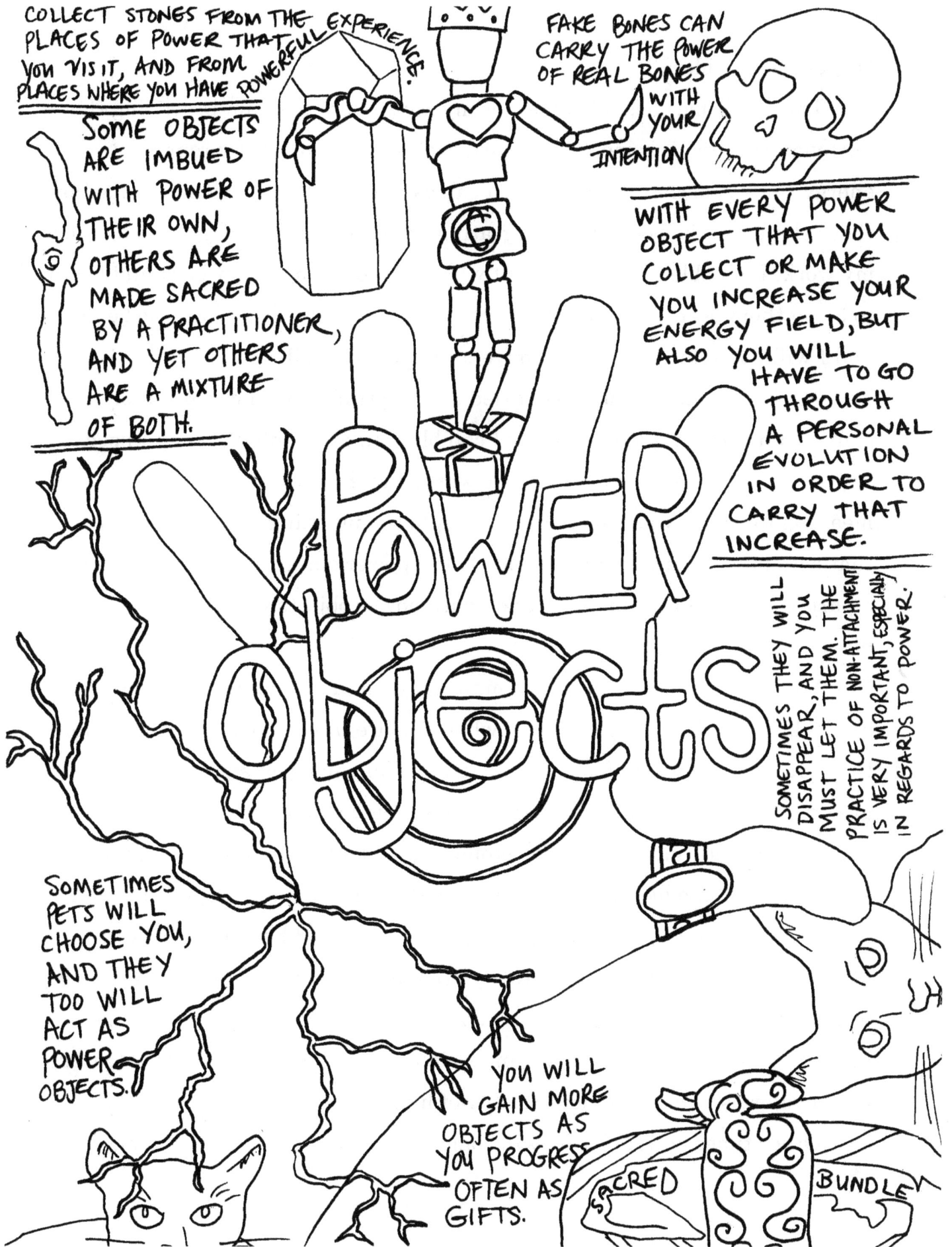

SACRED BUNDLE

Do you get the idea?

This medicine chest of stones, or my Mesa (because I am practicing the Peruvian tradition), is me, and in turn each stone that I carry represents an energy that resides in me, and that I can call on (or conjure with). By placing these stones on the body, and integrating them into one's energy field as I do my work, I am able to help clear out what is holding my client back and begin to bring them peace; to bring them into alignment. My client can also be me, and I will use stones to work on my energy field as well.

Working with a stone is as varied as everything else. I can put it on my body, I can carry it in my purse, or I can blow an issue into it, when I need transformation. Power objects can be worked with in any way that has meaning to you. If you can create a metaphor of meaning for an action, then that action has meaning, and intent. Every power object you have represents a part of you, and in your interaction with power objects you are able to bloom.

You will find power objects in many ways, and not necessarily when you are looking for them. Occasionally, when you are in need of a transformation that you are not aware of, someone will suddenly give you a gift. Know that gifts given to you for no reason tend to have a magickal reason and meaning. My mom recently gave me a fairy stone from Quebec. She said it reminded her of me, because looking at it there was the very apparent representation of a snake. I am currently working with its energies, and have it on my dream altar. I ask it to take me deep into my dreams to transform, and evolve. I also work with it to help me make contact with the fairy realm. I haven't work very much with the fairies, but I am excited to start to integrate their truths, and mysteries, into my understanding of life.

Other times power objects will come to you when you ask for them. When

I was in Australia I had looked for stones, but hadn't found any. I decided to purposely look for one, and had walked down to the bridge near a body of water to ask spirit, "Where is the stone that you want me to bring home? I have found no stones on my trip so far." I thought maybe I wasn't supposed to find a stone, and walked away from the bridge, losing myself in thought as I went back to the hotel. Suddenly I was taken aback to see a dead pigeon laying in front of me. I jumped, and exclaimed, "Oh my goodness!" and I thought, "What could the message be from a dead bird?!" And then I saw them, stones. A whole little area of stones gathered in one spot by one building. The only place I had seen stones in this place and on top of them was a dead pigeon. Death. I picked up the stone, and it looked to have rust on its underside; rust or dried blood. It made me very uncomfortable but I took it with me anyway. The spirit had shown me stones, and the bird had given its life so that I would notice. I thanked the pigeon and said a prayer over its body. It took me a year before I started working with that stone. I hadn't really realized that death made me so uncomfortable. Once the revelation occurred, I took that stone and added it to my altar, saying, "I accept the knowledge of death, even if it does make me uncomfortable, I accept your gift."

The death stone, as are all my stones, is a representation of an aspect of me. I hadn't actually consciously understood this until just right now (which is also another way in which magick reveals itself). I carry death with me, from the spider I kill out of fear, to the relationships I end in much the same manner (but not always). Death is a way of allowing the continuation of life, the ebb and flow of experience lending itself to the cosmic circle.

I found my lightning stone in Peru, on the sacred grounds of Saqsaywaman. I call it my lightning stone because it looks like a great bear, but has a white shape of lightening down the middle. The lightening breaks down from the head and into the bear's body. Lightning is a very important element for me. It also has special significance within the Q'ero tradition: to become an Altamesayoq (or one who speaks to the mountains) one must be struck by lightning, and survive. Lightning is significant for many reasons. The way that I was introduced to the archetype of lightning was from Don Mariano Quispe Flores, when I attended a workshop that he taught in Mount Shasta. In Quechua lightning is called illapa. Illapa is a powerful energy that illuminates, electrifies, and breaks through the darkness. This stone taught me the message of insight and the intensity of calling on lightning's energies. I do believe, however, that I also have a greater tendency to literally shock myself since I've been working with lightening.

I have two separate seeing stones, one I found on the beach in Costa Rica, and the other I found in the city of Pisac, Peru. Both are stones with holes in them. Seeing stones represent being able to see through the veil, seeing past the mundane to the spiritual world that lives right within it. I always wanted a stone with a hole in it, or as I like to refer to it: a 'holy stone'. When I was in Peru during my first visit I asked my spirit guides to bring me to a holy stone. I really wanted to find one just sitting there in the forest, but I would accept any holy stone really. I just wanted a holy stone.

The group's guide, that was leading us around the various sacred places in the sacred valley of Peru, brought us to a store in Pisac called 'the Shaman's Market'. There we found Apu stones (also called Chumpi stones), condor feathers, rattles and other various shamanic tools. Looking through the store I picked out some rattles that my teacher had wanted me to bring back for her, and various other tools. I wanted to get a

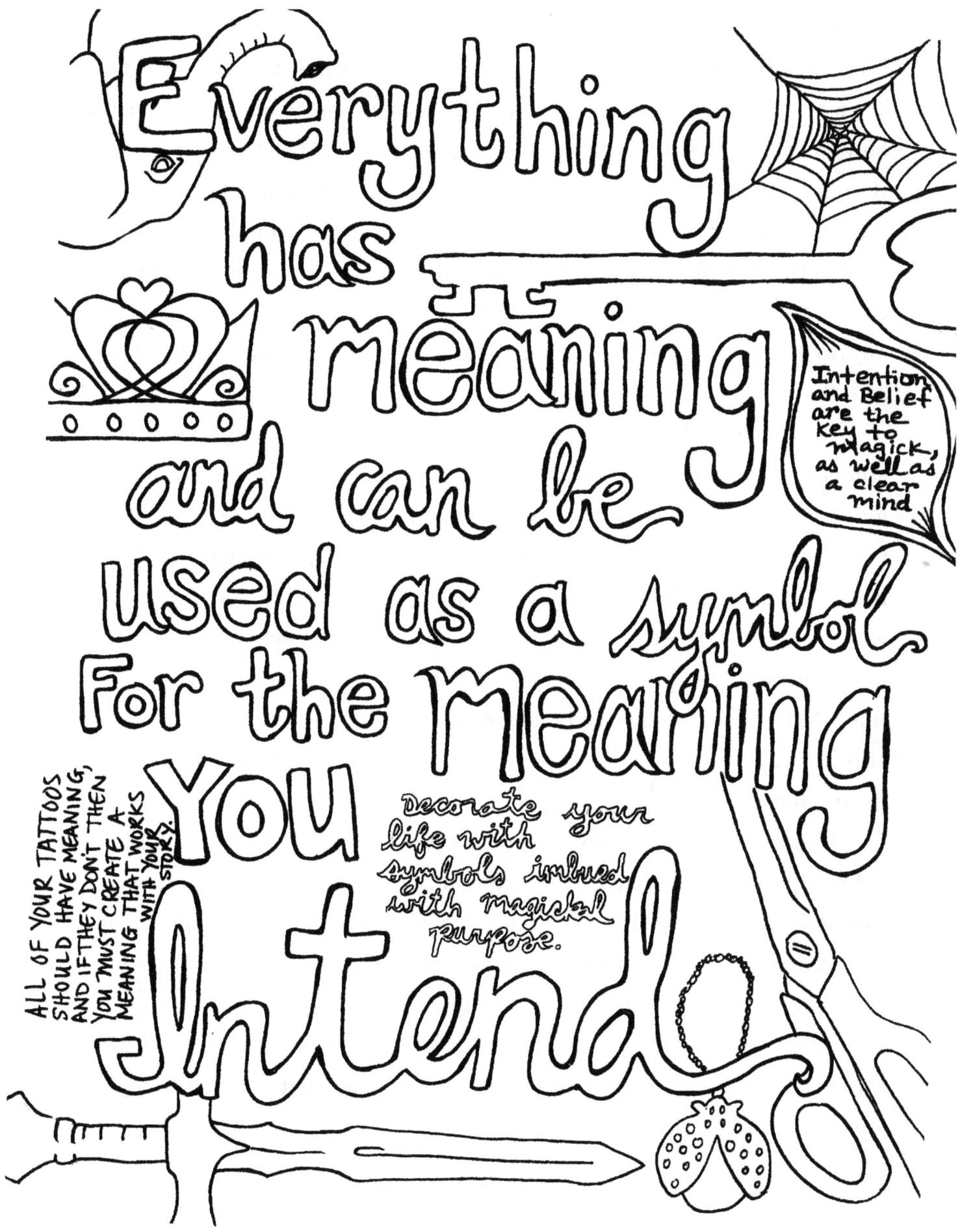

Everything has meaning and can be used as a symbol for the meaning you intend

Intention and Belief are the Key to Magick, as well as a clear mind

All of your tattoos should have meaning, and if they don't then you must create a meaning that works with your story.

Decorate your life with symbols imbued with magical purpose.

condor feather, but the pull wasn't strong enough for me to actually decide to. Then I came across a glass case, and my eyes were immediately drawn to the holy stone! A holy stone! I picked it up immediately, and looked at it thinking, "I covet you!" and then I put it back down. Something about the strength of my desire made me pause. I decided to look through the other stuff in the store first. I knew that I needed Chumpi stones that had been charged in the 12 sacred mountains of Peru. I asked the storeowner if he had any, to which he cocked his head and asked, "How do you know of this thing?"

"I study these practices, " I replied.

He then looked to our guide, and she assured him that I have been studying the Peruvian ways with a teacher. In my perception he seemed quite confused that I knew to call them Chumpi stones instead of Apu stones (Apu means mountain, and Chumpi means belt). To call them Chumpi stones is to refer to the initiatory practice they are used for: to install protective energy belts on a person's energy body, or the bands of power.

The owner gestured with his hand to the section of the store that was filled with Chumpi stones, and told me to choose. I looked to him and stipulated, "Yes, but I need a set that have been taken to the sacred mountains of Peru."

I can't really be sure why he had such a look of shock, but it was definitely shock at my request. The storeowner, upon my new stipulation, says that he has only three sets of sacred mountain charged Chumpi stones. He points the three out to me, and has me test their energy by waving my hand above them. I see the set I want, and feel the air above them. They resonate with me, with that electric magnetic sensation. I tell the owner that these are the ones I want, and decide in that moment that I need the holy stone too.

As he bagged it all up for me, he looks at me again with what I've now decided is a quizzical look, walks over to an assortment of meteorite and hands me one, "A gift for you."

I'm not really sure why he gave it to me, but I carry it on me in a medicine pouch most days, hoping one day I may understand its true meaning. Later, while reading a book on the Peruvian tradition, I found a passage that stated meteorite will protect a person from lightning. I imagine there will be other meanings as well, with the passage of time and the continuation of my journey, but I'm happy with this bit of information.

Know that your journey will require you to be a bit fluid with the truth of things. So much changes and mutates during ones' interaction with the mysteries, that it is mandatory to allow for such malleability. To try to hold on to one truth, unchanging, is to invite trouble.

The holy stone I found in Costa Rica was more the experience I had been asking the universe for before my visit to Peru. The funny thing about it was that I had stopped asking the universe for a holy stone because I now had one. I was in Costa Rica to participate in shamanic ceremonies, and we had taken a trip to the beach to relax and refresh ourselves. Walking down the sand to explore with one of the other participants I stumbled upon a holy stone. I picked it up immediately, excited that I was having the experience of finding a holy stone organically. I looked at it, and it looked like it was the shape of a head and the hole was where one of the eyes would be. I laughed to myself knowing this stone carried the mysteries of the ocean, where the other stone carried the mysteries of the forest, though this may change. With each power object that I work with I am aware that they may change their meaning, or power at any time.

Earthquakes are very important, and pretty regular in California. I found my earthquake stone at Mount Baldy, and though one might think that I found it during an earthquake, I merely found it on my way up the mountain. I didn't know it was an earthquake stone until months later, I just thought it was interesting, and felt it pull me, or call to me. I put the stone up to my ear and asked it what it represented to me, and then I felt my insides shake and I heard in my mind that this is an earthquake stone. The only way to begin to transform people is to shake and rattle their foundation, to bring an earthquake to their inner being, and so I use the earthquake stone to stir those energies, to break down boundaries, and to delve deeper.

I am also an earthquake, a shaker of foundations. That is the duty of the trickster and so also an archetypical energy that I carry. Just like Wiley Coyote, I am not only doing the trickery, I also get tricked all the time. The spirit world loves to trick me into a new journey, and seemingly that is the best way for me to learn. According to Carlos Castaneda's version of Don Juan Matus, one must always be tricked into the life of a shaman, or (hu)man of knowledge, and so trickery is a constant theme in the life of magick (Castaneda, 1968). I would like to state for the record that trickery is not a bad thing, as many people associate the word with bad experiences, or negative connotations. The trickster opens the door, and is the key-holder at the threshold. In order to disrupt the dominant way of things, one must shake them up, and so an earthquake stone is also an aspect of trickster.

You will find power objects and stones that work with you. Their power depends on your personal relationship with them, and your commitment to the workings. Sometimes, though, they don't need your attention, they are brought into your life to shift you, and bring you into a new level of awareness; they carry their own power.

In order for the greatest version of your shift to occur, you must continue to create a relationship, and to do the work.

When you work with your power objects you might find yourself singing, dancing, or otherwise moving energy. This is part of your communion with the energies that it carries. Ultimately you must trust your relationship with each power object, as they will have a specific meaning for you. I say this because you might come upon people who see your power objects, and claim that they do something else entirely. While this may be true, it may not be true for you at the moment.

I also have some power objects that I made myself. You can make a power object by creating something that is so tremendously imbued with your vision, intention, and power, that it becomes very powerful itself. These can sometimes be charged objects for spell work, but also you can create a figurine that represents you, and empower it in the ways that you want to create in your life.

Exercise in using Stones

You can work with stones as power objects pretty easily. Other power objects will take time to be introduced to your magickal journey. I want you to go out to the park or forest and look for a stone that calls to you. Calls to you can mean that it caught your eye, you feel drawn to it, or some other indicator that this stone wants to hang with you for a while. When you find that stone, I want you to lay down on the grass and put the stone either on your third eye, or hold it up to your ear. Ask the stone what it represents to you and then take several deep breaths. You will have feelings and memories enter into your mind; pay attention to these. This stone holds the lessons associated with those memories and feelings.

If you keep the stone in your sacred space at home, or on your altar, you will gain a greater relationship with it. Having stones that represent memories and feelings is very useful to seeing them from outside of yourself. The further you allow yourself to delve into the lessons surrounding them the more power you'll be able to gain from those experiences. Personal evolution is paramount to the magickal lifestyle.

11

Animal Spirit Guides

I wanted to call this chapter Animal Totems, because that is generally the terminology thrown around. I quickly realized that I don't really know much about animal totems in their true sense. This term stems from various cultures, throughout history, which I am not a part of. I do see, and appreciate, the current western idea that each person has an animal totem that they identify with, and that helps them understand themselves better, but this was not the traditional meaning of the term. Also, when working with animals, I find that there are many other ways that these beings will interact with the magickal practitioner.

As a means of staying away from a confusion of terms, I want to talk about animal spirit guides, and animals as guides. In my experience there are both individual animals, and archetypical animals, that will work with you. You can identify with an animal, and feel as if their archetype applies to you, but you don't have to decide on just one, and they will definitely change over time. When I was a teenager I identified as a gorilla, and currently I primarily identify as a wolf. I still harbor a soft spot in my heart for gorillas, but my primary animal identification is with the wolf. I imagine this may change in the future.

I attended a Christopher Penczak workshop at the Sacred Grove in Santa Cruz, CA (2006), wherein he taught us that we could have an animal team, as well as a plant team. I really liked the idea, and have kept it in my practice. I try to grow my plant team in my garden, and have representations of my animal team in my home. As time passes you may find that one animal no longer resonates quite as strongly as it used, or that new animals come into your life, and ask you to integrate their energies. This is all part of your personal evolution. We change throughout life, and so the way the universe interacts with us changes as well. Further, if you are engaging magick for

Engage With Your Spirit Guides

Seen and Unseen

out loud & psychically

They will help you even when you don't know you need HELP

You have many, and can gain favor with reverence.

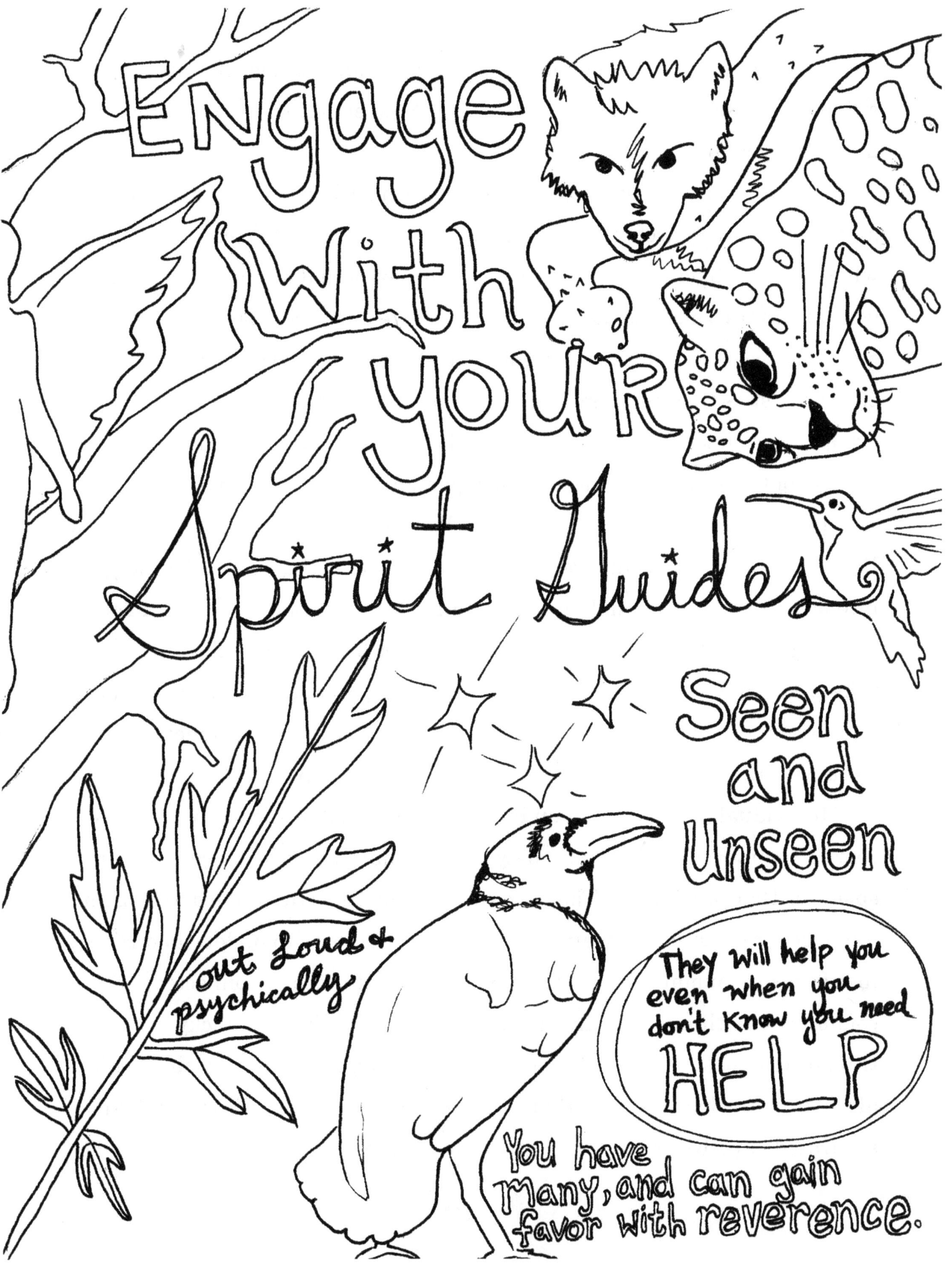

personal evolution, then you may have a more rapid change of animal spirit guides, because you will need to integrate those energies in order to bloom into what you are becoming.

The differences that I have found between archetypes and individual animals is that an archetype is more of a spiritual collective consciousness, whereas an individual is an interaction with an actual animal. The animal world is interacting with us constantly, and we only need pay attention to begin to receive the messages. Archetypical animals are the base characteristics that an animal group is known for; think of the apex of this group of characteristics as being the archetype. Individual animals will have aspects of the archetype, but express a personality all their own.

I work with archetypical animals when I need to change my perspective. If I need to see the big picture, I call on eagle, and will even invoke the spirit into myself and see through new eyes. If I want to work on weaving a spell, or weaving my world, then I will work with spider by calling on the energy to inform my spell work. I also have stones that represent various archetypes and I use these navigate through energy work. To call on an archetype is to work with the foundational spirit of that animal group.

Individual animals show up in the physical realm (though, there may come a time when I meet an archetypical animal in physical form, and I give space for that possibility). They come around at opportune times to bring a message, or insist you pay attention. How I have come to understand reality in regards to animal messages is that all living things are connected, and communicate, through the living matrix of energy. Think of sticky translucent goo, or threads connecting everything, like a huge web, that is alive. Humans have decided that we need words to communicate, and have separated ourselves from this matrix. Here's the kicker though, we haven't

actually separated, we've just collectively agreed on a willful ignorance. The plant world, and animals still communicate through the matrix of living energy. They are living their own lives, but are also very aware of all forms of communication. So, when I say that animals will give messages at opportune times, I am not suggesting that they exist for our knowledge, or further understanding. They are still living their own lives, but they are communicating in the unseen ways, and know how to give a message.

One day I was out doing errands, and I stopped into a diner for a late lunch. I was sitting at the table gazing outside, and being distracted in my thoughts when a raven walked across the parking lot. It was summer, and very hot, and I imagine the concrete couldn't have been comfortable. I've seen ravens walk before, that wasn't what took my attention, it was the length at which the raven walked: across the entire parking lot, and rather quickly, as if trying to get somewhere. I kind of laughed to myself and thought, "You're a raven! You can fly, why are you walking?!"

To which I heard in my mind, "Exactly Giana, why are you drudging through this stage of life, when you can fly?"

Now the laughter rolled in, as I realized the irony of my judgement. Raven had given me a message. I imagine this particular raven had a reason for walking, but we also connected through psychic communication, and I was granted a lesson, a message. This is how I work with animals: I pay attention, and try to communicate.

As you remember from previous chapters, interacting with animals is part of listening to the spirits guide. To work with animal spirit guides you can either ask to receive messages from animals, ask specific animals for messages, listen to animals communicating with you psychically, pray to archetypical animal spirits to create a change in your life, or to embrace

Make friends with your Fears

By acknowledging THEM

FEARS ARE IMPORTANT, THEY SHOW YOU PARTS OF YOURSELF THAT ARE DIFFICULT TO SEE. LOOK BELOW EACH FEAR AND FIND THE ROOT FEELING, AND THEN FOLLOW IT TO YOUR HIGHER SELF.

yourself, and new aspects of yourself. These are all ways to engage animal spirit guides, and I'm sure there are more. I like to interact with them in all of these ways, and am open to new ways emerging. The magickal lifestyle requires a state of malleability, or flexibility, from the practitioner. Life is not static, and it will not stay the same; either will your magick.

When I ask the universe for guidance I tend to get messages in response from animals. Now, for clarification, I say 'the universe' because it is a general question put out to the ethers, or cosmos, or collective energy matrix. When I ask specific deities, spirit guides, or beings for insight, I will be specific. Sometimes when I ask for clarification, humans will actually, literally, clarify something. When this happens, it is fun, and funny. Generally, though, I will have interactions with animals. When an animal shows up in response to a question sometimes it will be the scenario that has significance, and other times it will be the animal's archetypal symbolism that you will need to reference for your answer. I find that a scenario is a scene that occurs, or an animal doing something that has greater symbolic significance. If it's the archetypal answer, they will just be there, not doing much. Sometimes, it is both aspects.

If you'll remember from the chapter on Spirits Guiding, I told you a story of the eagle, the ravens, and the red-tail hawk. This is an example of a scenario animal message. An example of a archetypical answer would be the occasion of coming across a lizard. The lizard didn't do anything, and didn't run away, it was just there. When I saw this I went to a reference book on animal symbols and found that lizard are important to the dreamtime; to pay attention to dreams. When I look up meanings, generally the meaning that I need to see is what comes up, and at another time, with the same animal, a different meaning may catch my eye.

You can also ask a specific animal for guidance. Asking a specific animal generally requires a personal relationship with that animal. When I was trying to learn how to lucid dream, I asked my cat to help me realize I was dreaming in the dream time. That night my dream began as my sight came into focus, landing in the Amazon jungle in front of an Ayahuascero stirring his brew. My cat jumped into his arms from left frame, and he smiled, handing her to me. I responded that my cat doesn't usually jump to people, and that this was a rare occurrence, still fully immersed in the reality of the dream. I woke up, and apologized to my cat. Obviously I had more work to do because she had done everything she could to help me realize I was dreaming.

Listening to animals communicate is a fun practice. I am still working on this, and imagine I will for all of my life. When animals have communicated with me, they have done it with, what I call, word bubbles. Let me explain: I was sitting on the couch thinking about my roommate's cat, and why she wasn't as friendly to me anymore. She walked by me, looked up, and suddenly in my mind was an explanation. I call it a word bubble because it entered my mind all at once, not one word at a time. I looked at the cat, and said everything she sent me, out loud, feeling her explanation as I did. Satisfied that I understood her, we made peace, and she jumped in my lap letting me pet her. All animals can communicate, sometimes not with words, but with feelings, or pictures. Learn to listen, and they will speak to you more.

Calling to archetypical animals in your daily life, or in your magick work is a way of bringing specified energies to play. Sometimes when I am walking I will call on jaguar to walk on either side of me, or when I need to release an old pattern, I will call on serpent to help me shed my skin. Once you know the archetype of an animal, you can begin to work with that animal power.

Sometimes an archetypical animal will show up as a human. I once met raven, as a human woman. She attended one of my art shows. I titled the show, "The Trickster meets Herself: Finding Enlightenment by Falling on my Ass". The theme of the show was metaphysical; it was the story of my initiation into the mysteries of the universe. I had definitely fallen on my ass, and raven energy figured prominently into my experience.

Raven embodied by a human came to my show at the very end of the opening, and asked if she could have the crackers (I had set out cheese and crackers for the guests). She looked at my art, and then sat with me, not making much sense. Her black hair was tied back when she arrived, but as she was sitting, talking to me, she took her hair down. In that moment I recognized her as raven. Raven attended my art show. When it was time to leave, she was still there, and asked if anyone lived near her. She just *happened* to live a couple of blocks from me. I told her I would, but mind you I was little uncomfortable. Our chatter on the drive was nonsensical, and she directed me to a house that didn't actually feel like it was her house. I dropped her off, fully aware that she may have just disappeared into the night air. It was a bizarre experience, but it felt like raven appeared to validate the experience I expressed in my art show.

Identifying with an animal spirit, or what people tend to call animal totems, is a way of acknowledging and empowering specific aspects of yourself. Animals can represent parts of you, and you can identify with the lessons and perspectives of specific animals. This is invaluable in developing your strengths, and recognizing your weaknesses. I identify strongly with a team of animals. For me, having a team is how I recognize that I embody many, or different, energies. Sometimes I am very much a wolf, and other times I become a feline. Imagine this, a picture of yourself in the wilderness, and there are animals around you. Each represents you, and works with you because of that affinity. You may only see one or two animals right now, or you may see an entire team. Having a team is useful in self-understanding, but be aware that these tend to shift and change depending on where you are in your life. Allow for this fluidity in your practice, and accept the new spirits when they present themselves.

I have always needed to touch base with the animal world. Working at various office jobs through my twenties, and being the type to need more time with nature, I created a lunch break ritual. I would drive out to the nearest canyon or park in order to break away from the desk, and realign myself with the outdoors. On one such lunch break I took a walk in the park. Wandering and looking for signs, signs that reminded me of my magickal reality. Up ahead, I saw an area that began to shine; the misted light rays sprinkling through a circle of trees, a sacred grove. As I walked closer I noticed a raven feather, and picked it up. Then another, and another. The feathers were leading me on a path through the park until I was in the very center of the sacred grove. I looked down and saw that I was now carrying at least 30 feathers, and I knew they were instructions from the universe. I was to adorn myself with them. I was given a gift from an animal spirit that I work very closely with.

I wear feathers because raven works with me, grants me lessons, power, and secrets. Animal spirits guide, and lead the seeker into new vision, and knowledge. When you start interacting, and paying attention to, the animal world, you will begin to receive gifts. These gifts often lead you toward a relationship with an animal spirit guide that wants to work with you. Pay attention, and collect these gifts, as they usually become magickal tools.

Animal spirit guides are a powerful force. They bring archetypical energy and strengths to the practitioner that they choose to embrace. Listening to, and engaging animals, has changed my whole interaction with the world.

Here's a story that both illustrates how animals communicate, and also the possibilities of human consciousness. My sister's cat, a beautiful Maine Coon, who came into the family quite magically, told me a story once of what the difference between humans and animals is. Like most, I had assumed the difference is language, though I instinctively believe this finding is based in ethnocentrism. When cats talk to me they tend to look me right in the eyes and then I will have a thought pop into my head that is from the cat. My sister's cat looked me in the eye and said, "Humans are sad. They are sad, sad creatures, because they have so much possibility but they imprison themselves in their own perspective. The difference between humans and animals is that animals are what they are. A cat is always a cat. But a human can take on the perspective of the cat. They can be anything in this world, but they choose ignorance."

I was surprised by what she had told me, but it made sense. I knew that in the magickal lifestyle I had embodied different animals, and that this was possible, but outside of the magickal traditions this does not happen. Animals want to work with us because we are part of the living matrix of energy, interacting in the same spheres as them. They would prefer that we acknowledge this relationship, and communication.

Shadow Animals

I wanted to make a separate chapter on shadow animals, but realized this is an important aspect of this chapter and should be included here. In life, there are aspects of ourselves that we don't like. This is referred to as the shadow. When speaking of animal spirit guides I must also recognize shadow animal spirit guides, those animals we tend to fear, and who represent parts of ourselves we are uncomfortable with. A few of my shadow animal spirit guides are sharks, and black widows. I have dreams about both regularly, and for a very long time this was a source of great discomfort. In life, I am also literally surrounded by black widows. Wherever I move, so they appear at my front door, and in my garden. Working with shadow animal spirit guides is a way to acknowledge, and make peace with your fears, and yourself. For me, the shark is a predator, and I needed to acknowledge that ability within myself. I was speaking to a friend about this once, and she mentioned, "Yeah, they're predators, but there has to be blood in the water."

Whoa! This comment brought into focus the idea that one only attacks when the time for attack is right. Meaning, parts of me are predatory, but I don't attack for no reason. There has to be blood in the water. Blood in the water to me symbolizes the moment that attack is necessary. Sometimes when teaching concepts that are difficult to comprehend, the teacher must wait for the student to have a break in rigid consciousness, blood in the water, to bring the teachings of that concept.

This idea of a predatory nature was not easy for me to integrate. I don't think of myself as a predator, but obviously there are parts of me that will attack when necessary. Shadow animal spirits guides will show up in the dreamtime to alert you to their presence. This may be scary at first, but once

you start recognizing, and working with the energy, your dreams will become less scary.

I had a dream that I was on the beach with a woman, and she had bought a shark that was going to be delivered to the sand where we were. I think she thought it was going to be a great white because she kept mentioning that the plane to deliver the shark was going to have to be very big. When the shark was delivered, the plane was small, and it was a baby shark, about as big as a golden retriever. In the dream this shark could survive on land for a couple of days, but needed to have water eventually. I went over to the puppy shark and laid down next to it, cuddling into me like a cat. Like a puppy, the shark starts gnawing on my hands, but it doesn't hurt, and I'm not scared.

To accept the shadows within myself is to understand the workings of energy. Accepting the parts of myself that I do not like, as they exist, does not mean that I wish to perpetuate them, but rather that I acknowledge them. In the self-awareness and knowledge of one's own ability to give into their desires, and the reality of those addictions, takes the power away from them. Wanting to disassociate from one's own shadow only gives it more power over you. Do you hear me? If you try to oppress something inside you, it will gain power over you.

Shadow animal spirit guides are interesting, and I walk the line between being scared and fascinated. Meditating with spider is an interesting sensation. I did have an experience of becoming spider. The night that she came into my body, and let me feel the knowledge of her existence, was profound. I was lying in bed and my body pulsated and felt different than me. My skin became the skin of spider, and my womb became a producer of webbing. I am afraid of black widows, but I became black widow, and felt her intensity. She is the archetype and existence of death and creation. I became the small and powerful beauty that builds a home for the mate, a mate who would sacrifices their self to love; to the creation of life.

Spider and I have had a long, and tense connection, ever since my youth. I remember waking up in the middle of the night seeing big black spider on the ceiling above my head. Or the time I was talking to my mom in the kitchen and she looked at me in shock. My immediate thought was that there must be a snake behind me! (I find this hilarious). Nope, I had a spider crawl out from my shirt down my arm, and run back into my shirt for my mom to witness. I had not felt a thing, and would have never known had she not seen it. So many spider experiences throughout my life, and yet I never embraced them, only feared them more and more. When I began the magickal path I started redefining understandings that I held about reality, and spider was on that list. Over time I grew more and more comfortable with what spider's medicine carries, and the lessons she teaches.

Shadow Animal Spirit Guide Exercise

Getting in touch with your shadow totems is very, very easy. All you need to do is write down a list of the animals you fear the most. You can probably think of one or two animals that immediately send shivers up your spine. Now go look them up in a book or on the Internet to see what they represent. Do you resonate with what is written? I have found that the energy of a shadow totem is difficult to really comprehend because we are so uncomfortable with that part of ourselves that we oppress our own self-knowledge in that specific area. I know that for me, I had a real difficult time accepting that my shadow totems are deadly. Am I deadly? I can be, and my words can, and have, cut a person in half. Does that make me proud? No, not necessarily, but it is an aspect of me that can be utilized for a greater purpose.

Make a Shadow Animal Vision board

1. I know you're probably familiar with vision boards, and if you're not, quite simply they are a board filled with pictures of things you would like to bring into your life. When I was working through accepting my shadow totems I decided to make a Shadow Animal vision board, though, I put it in my Book of Shadows. You can do that as well, or you can do it on poster board, whatever feels right to you.

2. I printed out pictures of all the animals that scare me, and put words

next to them of what they represent. This was both scary, and invigorating.

3. Now I want you to meditate on each of those animals and think of something that is positive about them. For example, my friend told me that the black widow can be a wonderful metaphor for sacrificing yourself for love, really giving your entire being over to creation within love. That is powerful medicine! The black widow also really only comes out at night, so being able to see in the dark, and weaving your magick in the dreamtime! These are powerful attributes, and so I wrote those things down next to the pictures.

4. Once you are done with your Shadow Animal vision board you will spend ten minutes looking at your finished product, and then you are done with it! If it is in a place that you regularly look that is fine, but if it is put away in your book of shadows that is fine too. The real work was allowing yourself to spend time with the words and images that you would normally ignore and avoid.

Animal Spirit Guide Exercise

You may already be working with animal spirit guides, and you may not. I want you to pick your favorite animal. This a starting point, and for right now, it is your animal spirit guide.

1. Make an altar to your favorite animal. When I say altar in this context, I mean draw a picture, and frame it, or buy a picture and hang it, or get stuffed animal, or a figurine. Find an image of the animal, and put it in your living space.

2. You can build an altar to this image over time, as you come across more representations of your Animal Spirit Guide.

3. Put it in a place that gets attention. This will create a stronger connection for you.

Currently I have a spider pillow that I got around Halloween, reminding me to weave in my dreams, but also to help write this book. I have figurines of wolves, owls, ravens, dragonflies, and serpents all around my house. This is how I build, and maintain, connection and communication in my psyche.

12

Healing

There are many different forms of healing, and every cosmology has their own understanding of it. I believe that each one is correct, and valuable. The idea that only one tradition has access to the truth has never made sense to me. I don't subscribe to the belief that there is only one way. It seems only logical that every tradition, having come from its own understanding, will have found a form of healing that works. On the magickal path you must be continually working on your own healing. This is important, as a broken spirit will not do well with increased magickal proficiency, and power. I primarily have worked with a Peruvian energetic healing technique called soul retrieval, but also strive to integrate many different healing practices.

Soul retrieval can be done in many ways; each tradition will have their own particular technique. I have come to associate soul retrieval with a type of psychological therapy, wherein the healing taking place is psychological, and hopes to remove the emotional triggers from traumatic events. This aspect is the same, however, soul retrieval recognizes the emotional trigger as being psychological, and metaphysical. The energy body loses parts of itself during trauma.

There is disagreement as to where the soul piece goes, and how it feels, etc. In my perspective, when a traumatic event occurs, the soul piece breaks off and is stuck in that place. It may be hiding, it may be furious, it may be sad, it may be lost, but all in all it is no longer attached to the greater soul, or energy body. Soul retrieval's goal is to find the soul piece, disconnect it from the trauma, and bring it back into the energy body.

The most important part of healing is to transcend the victimization of life. If trauma constantly shades your outlook you will be a person of constant hurt, pain, and suffering. You know that you are in need of healing when you get triggered easily, when you are constantly framing your story from a place

Pursue Your
Healing
Always.

DO NOT BE AFRAID OF THE DARK

THE SPIRIT MUST BE IN A STATE OF CONTINUOUS EVOLUTION

IF YOU ARE UNAWARE of your trauma IT WILL TAKE Control of Your Magick

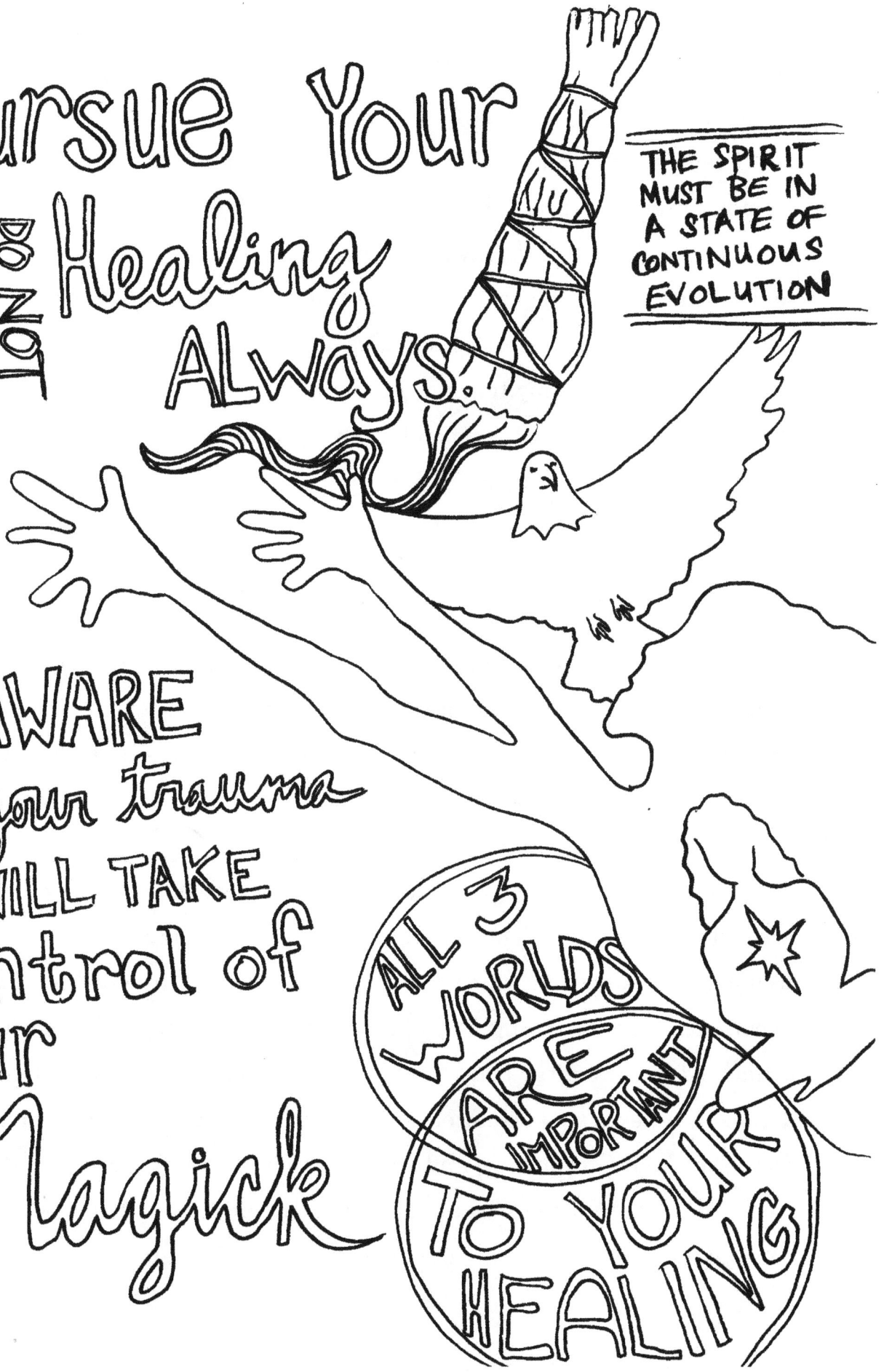

ALL 3 WORLDS ARE IMPORTANT TO YOUR HEALING

of victimization, or if you are suffering from a myriad of psychological maladies.

I remember having some early therapy sessions where I was guided to a memory, and then directed to imagine older self-comforting the younger memory self. This was, in my approximation, a form of soul retrieval. The real significant part however, is to cut the cords that connect the memory to the child, therein reclaiming its power. The way that I perform soul retrieval has come to me from my teacher, Esther Jenkins, as well as from spirit. The original technique that I learned has changed tremendously over the years, and through my practice. Spirit continues to guide me as I work with clients and I have found that my technique varies for each situation. If you want to learn more about soul retrieval, there are books, both by Peruvian authors, and anthropologists that detail the method.

Soul retrieval is very important for healing the energy body; it is a technique of reclaiming soul fragments from traumatic events in a person's life. The energetic body surrounds and engulfs the physical body. Once you have reclaimed many soul parts you will find that your aura, or energy body, is much brighter, and much stronger.

Thoughts are things. It is true, and the nature of your life follows the cycle of your thoughts. The way that I understand it is that soul pieces will fragment off during a traumatic experience, and continue to live in that experience, usually hiding from the trauma. These soul fragments are still connected to our energy body through luminous threads, and will dictate our actions whenever we encounter a situation that triggers that memory. These memories hold a frequency, and similar experiences will resonate at that frequency, triggering our trauma. When a trauma is triggered we react from this space, and are no longer ourselves, but a soul fragment reacting out of fear.

In order to reclaim soul fragments, we must journey to the underworld to face the memory. When we go back into a memory we bring our spirit guides with us, and in that memory we enter, at our current age, in order to save the soul piece, which many times is an inner child. When the child is saved the luminous threads that connect it to the memory are cut and we bring the child back into our body. The shaman that is performing the soul retrieval will energetically reconnect the child to the adult allowing reintegration.

In my meditation I have come to understand that this is an aspect of being in the now; if we have pieces of ourselves that are stuck in childhood, or stuck in past lives, then we too are stuck and not able to fully interact in the now. Being in the now is important in most spiritual traditions, and to come from a place of power seems to correlate with that type of being.

Healing is always ready to happen on the magickal path. Be open to having healing experiences without asking for them. While on a hike I was given an insight into my own healing, and a new tool to accomplish that healing. As a shamanic practitioner I have not been able to perform soul retrieval on myself, and have sought out the healing from my teacher. This is useful, and I would suggest it to other shamanic practitioners who are close enough to their teachers to do this. At a certain point, however, it is advisable to do your own soul retrieval, to embrace your power to a greater degree.

I love to hike, but had found for a handful of years that I would lose my breath quickly, and have to take many breaks. Hiking with a friend, who was an avid hiker, I noticed more and more that my breaks were significant. On one hike in particular, I asked her to stop, and held my hand to my chest, "I need to catch my breath," I told her.

"That's ok. Wait, are you having pains?" she was concerned.

"Yes. Yes, my chest feels as if it is constricting tightly around the center, and it hurts."

"Your heart rate must be racing," her concern grew, "Let's wait here for a while; take your time."

"It's interesting, I feel as if the tightness is a response to stress, as if looking at the hill makes me nervous, and then my chest tightens and I can't breathe. I feel as if it may be symbolic." I mused, "I feel better, let's continue."

As we continued it was only a minute or so later when my chest tightened again, "I need to stop," I said, breathing heavily. As I breathed, I focused my attention to my heart center, and asked, "Why are you closed, what pain are you carrying?"

In that moment I saw the memory of my first love, the memory of knowing she was cheating on me, and being unable to express my truth, or ask her about it. I felt stuck, sad, and cowardly. I felt as if I didn't know how to face this sort of truth. Then another memory came forward, and I saw a similar experience with the two girlfriends after her, one who was also lying and cheating, and the other who was just always mean. I could not stand up to either of them without entering into conflict, and I didn't know how to stand up to them. The tears began to stream down my face as I let my chest release this pain, let the energy work its way out, while re-envisioning myself standing up to all of them. "I must need soul retrieval for this," I thought, and as I thought it my spirit guides showed me a way in which I could perform soul retrieval for myself.

I looked around, and a saw a rock that caught my attention. Picking it up, I knew I would use it as a tool for this healing. I let myself feel all the pain, sorrow, fear, and cowardice that was welling up, and brought the stone to my lips, blowing out all that tension. I thanked the rock for its work, and put it down next to a tree, to mulch into the earth, and become compost for new growth.

I looked around, and found another rock, one that was pretty. I felt the earth energy swell, and visualized it seeping into me through my feet. I felt my connection to the power, and imagined myself admitting the truths that I saw. My trauma had been from knowing a truth, but being afraid to see it. My power was in the knowing; I always knew. I thanked the universe for the experience that I had just had, and blew all my love, joy, and confidence into this new rock. I kept this rock, and walked away, not looking back. The first rock took my heavy energy, and allowed me to cut ties with it. The second rock became a symbol, first, of this spontaneous healing experience, and secondly, of my courage, love, and passion. With every pain, there is a power to be claimed.

Soul retrieval is not the only healing technique out there, every tradition has one, at least. I consider Yoga to be a healing technique. I have also found that in your healing, you will need to integrate some sort of stretching practice, and Yoga is a good one. Energy builds up in your body, and you must stretch in order to process it out. I find that having a continuous Yoga practice is in itself a practice in discipline. Now, I state that you need to have a practice of stretches, but also, full disclosure, I often fall off the wagon of stretching, and I feel the difference. Just know, moving the body is part of healing.

One good healing practice, that is actually more of a continuous cleansing, is to do an uncrossing spell every month. Thoughts are things, and people are, well, people, who have bad thoughts. These sometimes build up in our energy field, and it's nice to have a monthly cleansing ritual where you

Physical Action is important to your Magickal Practice

SOMETIMES YOU MAY FIND IT HARD TO GET UP THE ENERGY TO MOVE, BUT THAT IS WHEN YOU MUST

STAGNANT ENERGY CREATES SICKNESS WHEN MUCH MANA IS ACQUIRED.

MOVE YOUR BODY

STRETCHING HELPS MOVE THE ENERGY OUT OF YOUR BODY

SOMETIMES IT IS NECESSARY TO HYBERNATE, BUT STILL TRY TO DO YOUR STRETCHES AT NIGHT TO RELEASE THE PENT UP ENERGY

Be sure to integrate a regimen into your daily physical activities break any, and all, bad stuff that's come your way. You can use a yellow candle, with an uncrossing sigil, that you light along with copal, and chant for inner peace; lighting the way, and clearing your path. Or, you can use a black candle, with a protection sigil, that you burn with sage, and chant that negativity be absorbed, while you chant a mantra of grounding; clearing out all muck, and sending it to the fiery core. You get the gist. Make a date, set a reminder, and keep your magickal space clear.

There are so many healing practices to choose from, and you can choose all of them if you'd like. Healing is the primary focus in the magickal lifestyle, because a witch needs to be coming from a place of strength, and solidity when practicing magick. Some people with disagree with this, but in my belief, you must pursue your healing with diligence. You must be of strong spirit when you garner power.

Getting regular massage sessions can help you move the energy build up in your body. Self-care is an important aspect of healing, and should be engaged in regularly. To keep your energy field clean, and strong, be sure to take a salt bath after a healing session. I am also particularly fond of going out to a mountainous, or forest, area and finding a stream of water. To get energetically clean, you've got to take off your shoes, and let your feet *feel* the soil. This is your connection to the earth, and to releasing any heavy energy. Natural moving water is a wonderful source of charged cleansing energy. When you are cleaning yourself, imagine all your heavy energy releasing out of the souls of your feet, and bringing in the powerful earth energy to fill you. The earth controls growth, and in the growth cycle decomposition becomes nurturance for new growth, and as such your heavy energy goes away to become a power source.

In every tradition that I have practiced, or trained in, there has been a healing. I cherish all of my healing experiences, and find they weave into the tapestry of a magickal journey. Each of my tattoos actually represents a magickal experience, and subsequent healing. Going to Italy to dance and drum the Tarantella was magick, but it was also healing. Attending medicine ceremonies, sweat lodges, and rituals were all about magick, and healing. There is no way to get around it, and if you practice this path you *must* endeavor to heal yourself. I have heard it said that the shaman is the wounded healer, and it would seem that the archetype of the witch, the shaman, the sorcerer, is a person that others seek out when they are in need of help. You cannot heal others if you don't heal yourself.

If your practice is not about healing, but rather about power, and control, I want you to question why that is. Many times a person will endeavor power, when they come from the trauma of being powerless. What is the root core of why you want to practice magick? If it is for malicious intent, you will self-destruct, and it will be because you never engaged healing.

Healing Exercise

Healing can be easy, and soothing, at times. One really effective healing technique is a salt bath. Salt is used in many magickal traditions as a protector against negativity; bad things cannot pass salt without being purified. So, we put salt at our doorsteps, and under our windows, when protecting a home. We are energetic beings, and maintaining a clean energy field doesn't necessarily come naturally to us. A salt bath is a wonderful way to clean the excess energy gunk off, and is wonderful for the body.

1. Fill the tub with your favorite temperature of water

2. Throw in a cup or two of salt. (This is really personal preference

though. Do as much as you'd like).

3. Steep yourself

4. (Optional step) Going one step further with this healing bath, you can put flower petals in the water with you. Make sure you're not picking poisonous flowers, otherwise, flowers have a beautiful energy, and you can utilize them to re-inform you energy field with their essence. Salt clears it out, flowers brings it in.

5. Candles are nice too, but not necessary.

13

Plant Medicine & Altered States of Consciousness

She went
to my
submerged
cave
of broken
bones,
fleshless
bodies,
Treasures.

Flooded it.
my whispers
floating
to the
surface,
drench
my
sight

If you take nothing else from this book, know that you must speak to the spirits. Do not let that worry you if you feel you are not equipped; you are always speaking to the spirits, however sometimes you must try harder, listen deeper, and make a ritual of it. Often times I find myself impatient with the spirits, wanting to know more, wanting to go now, wanting, wanting. This has only caused me worry and sorrow. The spirits speak when it is time, and you listen. Living the magickal lifestyle is not about control, it is about being in flow, in communication, with all the magick around you.

The plants are spirits, and they too need your attention. I would actually say that you need theirs, to feed your spirit, body, and soul. There are different ways to speak to the plants. You don't necessarily need to eat, drink, or smoke something, but you can. I will cover both working with the plants with ingestion and without. I highly suggest working with plants without ingesting them first, as it will help you familiarize yourself with their personalities.

I have planted a magickal garden, in that the plants in my garden are allies on my magickal journey. Over time, you too will find plants that you feel more drawn to than others. Work with them, talk to them, feel them, and allow yourself to create a relationship. Plants will help you in your magick, both by talking to you, and by granting their energy to your incense mixtures. I have found, when I have a particularly strong affinity for the medicine of a plant, that just having it at my front door alters the consciousness, or perceptions of reality, of everyone that passes its threshold.

Now, plant medicine and altered states of consciousness are not the same thing, however, they are sometimes woven together. I am of the belief that all of magick will engage you in an altered state of consciousness, and plants have their own special place in that mix. Most people in society associate altered states with drugs, which come from plants, and so I will put them together, but know they are not the same thing.

I define an altered state of consciousness as experiencing non-ordinary reality. Ordinary reality is the day to day, the mundane, the worry of to-do lists, and gossip, and consensual reality with the dominant culture. Every day we consent together as a people to experience the same type of reality, and in that way we have interactions that are *expected*. I can feel the rhythm of my day influenced by the rhythm of everyone's expectations of the day. We consent to reality. To disengage with dominant reality, to step outside of expectations, is to enter non-ordinary reality, to alter your consciousness. This is not just doing something out of the norm, but to disengage with the normal consciousness.

When I was in community college I took an Anthropology of Magick and Witchcraft course, and one of our assignments was to use drumming to alter our consciousness. I can't remember the specifics of what was expected, but I remember vividly closing myself in my room, lighting incense, and drumming. I tend to want to be secretive, and at this point in my life I had never really given myself over to full expression. In my room, alone, I was allowed to lose myself in creating a rhythm, a communion, with this drum. It was an invaluable assignment. Now, in my magickal practice, I find that giving myself over to the spirit of expression is to alter my consciousness, to become one with the creation and with the act of feeling. It is a sense of leaving my body, and becoming one with the moment.

There are many ways to alter your consciousness, and on the magickal journey this is very important. Dance, singing, meditating, and chanting are all very fun, and profound ways; I would recommend trying a bit of everything until you find what really sets you into your groove, and maybe *they all do.* I also love to work with plants. Again, I'm not going to tell you how to prepare and imbibe plant medicine, but I am going to tell you how to alter your consciousness with them.

Plant your own magickal garden, and spend time in that garden. Plants communicate, and they can alter your consciousness just by sitting in their presence. I do not have a natural green thumb. It has taken me thirty years to learn how to listen to plants' needs. I tended to either over water, or under water, my plants, and they would die. I couldn't understand how other people knew how to keep plants alive. I reflect on this with laughter. Water is associated with emotion, and arguably my early relationships ended because I was too clingy (over watering), or I wasn't emotionally engaged (under watering). As I have grown in my spirituality, I have developed a greater understanding of balance, and how to listen to plants when they tell me what they need.

I go out into my garden, and I ask the plants, "How y'all doing?" and then I listen. They way to listen is to feel, that is how plants communicate. You must open yourself up with your question, and then pay attention to the feelings you get.   Ok, so that's how you build a relationship, and start talking to plants. Further, you want to have a team of plants to work with in your magick, and in order to augment their efficacy, you need to listen to them. Think of it as a courtship. You need to court magickal plants to see if they want to work with you magickally, and you need to pay attention to their consent. Once a plant has agreed to work with you, their essence will affect your consciousness. Arguably, plants will affect your consciousness when they want to, but if they work with you then it is more of a mutual endeavor.

Working with the spirits of plants keys you in to their particular personalities, or resonance. You will begin to learn from the plants what they do, and how they affect the world around them. By spending time with them you can then learn how to work with them, and how they will affect your consciousness. Altering your consciousness is utilized as a means of learning, or affecting change on the spiritual realm. When you have a specific purpose, you will know which plant to work with. Spend some quiet time with that plant; sit in its presence. How do you feel? If you're new to *feeling,* go find a book or online reference and look up the metaphysical uses or meanings of the plant. With this added information, you can then go see if the plant feels like the attributes your research had reported. In this way you create a communion.

Meditating is another way to alter your consciousness, and to do this with plants will help foster your communication with them. Remember, in the beginning there is a tendency to dismiss thoughts that come into your head as 'just your imagination'. Strike that phrase from your lexicon. Imagination is a crucial aspect of the magickal lifestyle, but also not everything is your imagination, you were just taught that it was. When I talk to the plants I will often imagine their responses in my head, and most times I will feel/hear a clear response. Many times they will have distinct patterns of speech, or dialect, a certain turn of phrase. It may be the way I imagine them saying something, but they're are still saying something, and they want me to listen. I always gain insight when I allow myself to listen.

When I am doing spells I often make my own incense, and a good practice to have is gathering your own plants. I keep a book on magickal correspondences of plants near my altar at all times, and utilize plants that resonate with the work that I'm doing. Gathering in the wild was actually a really difficult practice for me, because it is appropriate to ask the plant if you can harvest it's leaves and flowers. I had been too impatient to ask, or to

FEAR IS A TRAP

IT STARTS AS A self preservation mechanism, but develops into a Blockage from Revelation. You Must face your fears each time they appear.

IT DOESN'T MATTER WHAT YOU FEAR, ONLY THAT YOU ADMIT TO IT, AND STRIVE TO FACE THEM. FACING YOUR FEARS WILL NOT MAKE THEM DISAPPEAR, BUT IT WILL GROW YOUR COURAGE

ANYONE WHO SEEKS TO PUT YOU IN FEAR IS TRYING TO TAKE POWER OVER YOU

WE ALL HAVE FEAR

Courage feeds the Soul

allow for an answer. I wanted the plant, and I was going to take it. I want you to really let that sink in. I was enacting a very Western mindset, and honestly the plants did not appreciate it. When you harvest, you must always ask if you can, and leave an offering in return. Water is generally a safe bet, but listen to your intuition.

Incense will alter your consciousness. Each incense has a specific intention set by the plants used to make it, but it can also be used to trigger you into alternate reality. When I first started learning Wicca, Cindy told us that we would begin every magickal class by burning sage. She told us we were using it to clear each other's energy bodies, but also the smell of sage was being associated with *magick time*. Now, whenever someone burns sage I am immediately in an altered state, ready to engage in magick. It's a bit of magickal function, in that sage actually does cleanse the area, but also Pavlov's dog, in that the association triggers an immediate response.

Talking, and listening, to plants is in itself a form of altered consciousness; society doesn't generally allow the practice without questioning sanity. Plants are very efficient at altering your consciousness, and as a magickal practitioner it is beneficial to have them as allies. Work with the plants that call to you, first, and then branch out over time. Different plants will come into your life at different times, and their appearance is always purposeful.

Imbibing Plant Medicine

Plant medicines, or teacher plants, are highly controversial in western society, and many times they are just plain illegal. In many other cultures teacher plants are highly valued, and considered powerful healing teachers. There are so many books, both academic and experiential, that detail the history of teacher plants. Seek those out, and find out the specifics. I work with plants, in my garden as I have explained, and also in ceremony through ingestion. I believe there is much healing and knowledge to be gained in both ways of communion.

I have worked with a handful of teacher plants, and Ayahuasca was one that I felt a strong affinity for. Occasionally when working with spirits, a practitioner will feel as if they are married to a particular one. This has happened to me twice (thus far): Mount Shasta, and Ayahuasca have both told me that we are married. Marriage in spiritual terms is a little different than society's understanding. Also, depending on what tradition you are working with, there will be different definitions of being married to a spirit. In my case, with Aya and Mt. Shasta, it is more of a spiritual intertwining; I belong to these spirits, they are a part of me, or as if their spirits live in my spirit. Now, when I say that I am married to Ayahuasca, please understand that I am not an Ayahuascera. I was given an understanding by the spirit of the plant, and I hold that dear, and to be true, but I have not been officially trained in the medicine.

Ayahuasca is a sentient spirit, a being, a healer. In the way that I know her, she is a type of dark goddess, a serpent that will take you into your deepest, darkest places, and shed light. For those who approach her with reverence and respect she will guide you through profound healing. Well, she's going to heal you no matter which way you come, but I prefer to be deferential. She is also a mother that knows that some lessons are not easy, but must be faced. A sort of tough love situation, with extra emphasis on the love. You don't necessary need to work with her in sacred ceremony to meet her, you can talk to her spirit in the Cappi vine. Like all plants, you can speak to them without ingesting, however, it does help to be in the plants presence.

To illustrate an experience of Aya, I have detailed one ceremony that I experienced below, but be aware that not everyone will have the same experience. I want to introduce you to her medicine through my anecdotal story, but know that she almost always defies what you think is going to happen, in order to take you into what you need.

In my experience with Ayahuasca I did not have amazing visions of cosmic beings coming to take me home, and actually I barely had visions at all, except in my mind. My experiences in ceremony were so completely monumental to my spiritual journey, however, that I consider Aya the most gracious and loving of dark teachers; a woman who is not to be disrespected, but can illuminate personal transformation for those who come to her in earnest truth and humility.

Ayahuasca Ceremony #1

It was an hour and a half before 'la medicina' began to take effect, though you could say she had been in effect, but it took a long time to find the depths of my sickness. When I did begin to have a physical experience of Aya she came to me as a snake in the visions that appear with eyes closed. Dots and Lines were moving, many snakes were slithering, my purge bucket was surely filled with vipers waiting for a feast of darkness, and the ground under my hands slithered like snakes making me feel unsteady. Nauseous. I was not afraid; I knew Ayahuasca comes through as a snake to many people. My body then engaged in what I can only describe as the belch/yawn war. I had once eavesdropped a conversation when I heard, "When working through emotional issues if one begins to yawn it means there is a deep seated emotion that doesn't want to come out". I found myself yawning as if I could swallow all of the earth's air in one gulp, and then immediately belching a deep guttural rumble, that when keeping my mouth shut (to keep the noise down) sounded as if I was conjuring/calling to the toad people (as was later described to me by my Ayahuasca roommate). This war went on for at least fifteen minutes, and I knew that I wanted to get the poison out. Then I could feel Ayahuasca, who became Sachamama (the great serpent of the jungle, so big that when she moves the jungle falls) in my vision, coming up from depth of my belly, rising through my esophagus, and as she came whispering, "well you hid that deep, didn't you?"

In my head I had been unknowingly repeating a mantra, "I don't want to keep it hidden anymore, I want to let it go", and the voice saying it was my younger self. The vomit felt like a snake head in the back of my throat and it was as if some part of me was afraid to purge it, but Aya being a divine mother, and healer, gave me a nudge and I purged, and purged, until the poison was gone. As I purged I saw a vision of my mom and dad, and this picture suddenly ripped apart but then came back together, my soul felt as if it had been hit by an earthquake, my foundation shifted. As the picture separated I was overcome with the emotion I had never allowed myself to experience, grief and sorrow. My parents' divorce. I was mourning a loss that I had never mourned, grieving the pain that I had never acknowledged. I was given a moment, where the picture came back together and I relived a memory of my mom, dad and I in the house where I grew up, and I was allowed to relish in the joy that I had there, and allowed to mourn that the family unit had dissolved.

Then I had a conversation with Sachamama, and I noticed that my entire body had a minty, tingly, lightness to it, as if the weight of suppressing my feelings had lifted, and my body didn't understand gravity without it.

BREATHE

Open up and
Eviscerate
Everything.
Breathe into
Your Darkness, darkest
parts, Bring a fire
to your Heart

So That You
May Know
Yourself.

& BREATHE

The next morning, I had difficulty walking. I was light, lighter than my body understood, and my center of gravity was off because of it. I asked others, "Are you having difficulty walking? My legs feel so light." No one knew what I was talking about.

Ingesting plant medicines will definitely alter your consciousness in a very immediate way. In my experience with Ayahuasca I felt I had healed parts of me that I did not realize were in pain. When my parents got divorced I was happy because they were miserable together, and that joy in the function of shifting out of a poisonous home life overshadowed the reality that I still needed to heal.

In subsequent Aya ceremonies I have come to revere 'la medicina' as a powerful ally in healing the spirit of mankind. As I write this, I am reminded again that altering your consciousness is to engage with the spirit world for a purpose; my purpose is generally healing. Not all magickal practitioners engage in this same way; some will alter their consciousness as a means of gaining power. Do not engage in that path. The quest for power almost always comes from trauma; do not let trauma lead your life story.

As a witchy shaman, or magickal practitioner, you will need to get very good at altering your consciousness at will. To engage in alternate reality is to work directly with magick. Find a technique that works for you, and practice it. Once you *know the feeling* of altered consciousness, it is easier to recall it, and enter into it. Just feeling the shift will enter you in to it. Altering your consciousness allows you to see what is not normally seen, hear what others don't, and enter into the dance of the ethers.

Altered States of Consciousness Exercise

You don't need to go to the jungles of Peru in order to engage in life altering consciousness shifting. Not everyone is called to work with plant medicine. Everyone on the magickal path is called to alter their state of consciousness, however, and drumming (as well as rattling) accomplishes just that. In order to make this work, you must find a way to let yourself go into the sound of the drum.

1. Find a quiet place

2. Burn your favorite incense.

3. Begin to drum a beat (you don't necessarily need a drum for this exercise, though it would be preferable)

4. As you are drumming, there is a desire to control what you are doing. Let go of control, you don't need to worry about doing it wrong, or not being good at drumming

5. As you let yourself go, I want you to begin to change your rhythm. Follow the drum, not your mind

6. Once you hit 'the sweet spot' or the drumming rhythm that really feels like you are in touch with the spirit, go with it. Don't stop until you feel it is time to stop. In the repetition of the drum your consciousness will feel free and safe to wander off. Follow it into the great unknown!

Altered State of Consciousness Exercise #2

Mugwort is one of my favorite plants. I consider her an ally, and a friend. If you look up her medicinal properties you will find she has many uses for physical ailments, but I know her as a psychic aid. In magick books you will find recipes for Mugwort washes that you use on your divination tools, and some people sleep with Mugwort under their pillows (both of which are excellent practices). I like a little Mugwort tea to alter my consciousness. Mugwort is subtle, but will shift you in to altered consciousness very easily.

I prefer to grow my own Mugwort, and use those leaves for the tea, but in a pinch your local metaphysical shop will carry Mugwort in their herb section. I've even seen that some places carry Mugwort tea bags. However, you are able to get it is fine.

1. Set your space with magickal intent. Do you want to talk to your spirit guides? Do you want to meditate? Focus your space so that you're not focusing on it while in altered consciousness.

2. Brew your tea. I find it soothing to hum or sing while heating the water, and preparing the brew. Singing brings you into an altered state of consciousness as well, so you will be funneling all of your focus into the magick of the moment.

3. Sit in your sacred space, and drink your tea.

4. Once you've finished your tea, I want you to engage in your magickal endeavor. Meditate, or visualize, or spend time with your plants. Notice how you are feeling, and how other things feel. You will find that you are more sensitive to the vibrations around you. You have successfully altered your consciousness using a completely legal plant medicine.

Altered State of Consciousness Exercise #3

This exercise is meant to tap you into the unknown, and out of yourself. There are many ways to alter your consciousness, but again, once you know the feeling, you will be able to do it at will. Each of these exercises is working towards getting you to experience a version of the feeling.

1. Go to a place where you will not be interrupted, and where you feel safe.

2. Close your eyes, and open your mouth.

3. I want you to explore your own sound. You may not think you can sing, but I don't care. You need to learn the sound that is yours.

4. Start with a hum, or Om type sound, and then let the sound lead the way.

5. After a little while you will feel yourself being led to knew vocal expressions. Follow, follow, follow; you are going into the depths of yourself.

6. Practicing this enough will bring you to a point where singing actually takes you out of your body, and in connection with alternate consciousness.

With each of these exercises, you will begin to feel the difference between normal reality, and altered consciousness. Once you are familiar will the feeling, you will be able to shift your consciousness at will.

14

Bad Magick

At first, this chapter was going to be a lot of finger wagging. I felt sure of my understandings of bad magick, and what can be considered good or bad. Bad magick is actually not that easy to define, as there are many circumstances that can transform a situation into an ambiguous definition. In magick, if you search out for power you will be tempted to the bad side of magick. Bad magick, is, well, bad. People tend to call it black magick, and I try not to use that term because I feel it can lend to racist ideation. I also try not to use the term negative magick, because negative energy and positive energy are just different ebbs and flow. The way I understand it, negative energy is actually feminine, in that it takes in, whereas positive energy is masculine because it projects out (think electrical circuits). With all that being said, let's define bad magick, which is magick that is used to overcome another human's willpower. I have also found that magick becomes bad when the intent is based in ego, or from a place of fear, rage, hate.

On occasion, I have been told by other practitioners that to do magick when you are full of rage is very powerful, and a good place to source from. I disagree. I think that if a practitioner needs rage, fear, or hate to pull from in order to cast magick that works, then that practitioner has a lot of healing to do. If you find yourself in a situation where you want to turn to bad magick, take a deep breath, take a jog, do something else to expel that energy, and then return to the problem at hand. All situations can be dealt with through courage, love, and light. If you can train your emotions to not take you over, and can come from a good place when casting your magick, then you can become a very wise and powerful practitioner.

The way that I understand magick is that you are bringing energy through yourself, and projecting it out into the ether. If you project good energy, focused on healing, evolving, or changing, your energy field is affected

Do Not Conjure to force Truth from Someones Lips, stand in your Knowledge of truth and it will Reveal itself.

Live in your truth without reserve.

When you have faith it in the truth it comes forth.

by that resonance. If you send out bad energy, focused on anger, rage, or hurt, you are similarly affecting your energy field. I have heard that it is possible to send out magick without having its energy affect your field, by disconnecting with the energetic output, but I haven't seen any personal examples for reference.

The best magick you can do is to cast upon yourself. When you want to change something in your life chances are that you really want to change yourself. This is good magick. This is working with magick to evolve mind, body, spirit. When you want to change something and you attribute that 'something' to someone else, and then decide to cast against them, you are practicing bad magick. You will experience the pain of overtaking someone else's will, trust me. Do not practice bad magick, it has a sticky residue that you conjure through yourself as you project it out. That residue will create physical, mental, and spiritual problems for you.

There is also the instance in society where a great evil is arising, or being perpetuated against groups of people. There is a difference between using magick to overcome someone's will, and using magick to right a wrong. You could argue that what is considered right or wrong changes over time, and I would agree; human consciousness is constantly changing. I am not going to write a treatise on what is considered good or bad. I have to trust that each practitioner will be self-aware enough to make that decision on their own. In the moment that something is wrong, and needs to be corrected, you can work with the spirits to intervene. If you make a strong case for injustice, the spirits will work swiftly.

As a point of contention I want to speak a little about conjuring the truth. At some point you may become philosophically involved with whether or not to conjure the truth from someone's lips. I believe in the truth, and that it should come to light, especially if people are being harmed by lies. It is a bit of an ethical quandary, however, whether or not to use a potion on someone to force truth from their lips. Be warned, not only will the responsibility of forcing the truth be carried by you, but your own truth will undoubtedly be exposed as well. If you are relying on lies, they will be unmasked.

Do not be surprised if the truth is not what you realized. It is best to let the truth stand for itself. It is a virtue and it exists outside of you. Stand in your knowledge of the truth, with all of your might stand strong in that knowledge. Generally, when the point comes for you to want to conjure the truth it is because you believe the truth is being hidden. The truth wants to be revealed. Standing confidently in your knowledge will allow for it to reveal itself. To force someone's truth as a means of taking power over them, is a form of bad magick.

Bad magick isn't solely confined to witchcraft. Focusing intent on bad feelings and sending them out is a bit of bad magick, and anyone can do it. Living in Santa Cruz and apprenticing at the local witchcraft shop, I learned many idiosyncrasies of the witchcraft society. Not only was I able to see buying patterns, but I also witnessed who came into the shop. Sometimes the most unassuming person would come in looking for love spell ingredients. Love spells are not inherently bad magick as long as the technique focuses on bringing love into your life, and teaching you to love yourself, so that you will be ready for love when it arrives. Not everyone realizes this, and sometimes people will try to force another to love them by employing magick. I have seen many people do bad magick, and it's not necessarily the 'ugly old hag' you might stereotypically expect.

Apprenticing was a quick acclimation process, most customers that visit

DO NOT EVER RECAST from REGARD

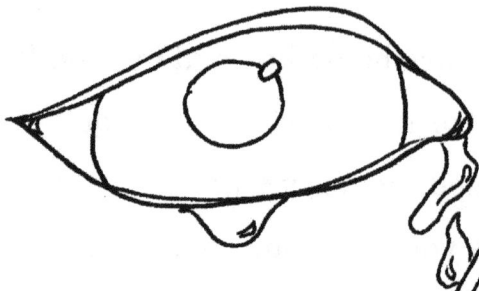

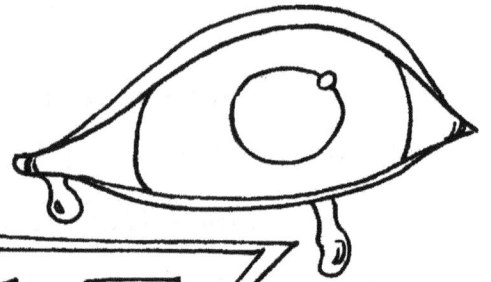

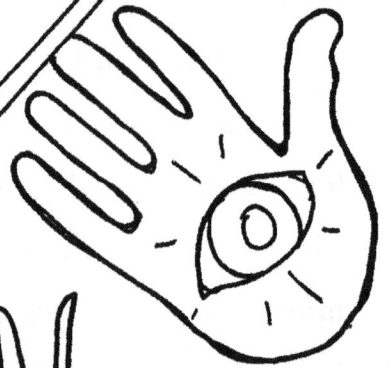

NO GOOD DECISION WAS EVER MADE IN RAGE AND ANGER.

Follow That Feeling to its core, and process your pain. Then Decide your course of action.

Lead with your Heart

However, It is never acceptable to allow someone to Harm you. You make boundaries and stick by them, And become very good at protective magick!

You Don't like The Feeling, So don't manifest MORE

a witchcraft shop will ask which ingredients are good for different purposes, and it is assumed if you work there that you know. Many times there would be no customers and I would make myself busy restocking the herb jars, or perusing our book selection.

It was there that I came face to face with opposition as well. What better way to find witches than to go to a witchcraft shop, right? And find us they did; the seemingly homeless man who made a point of harassing us at least once a week, once even loudly proclaiming I was possessed by wolf-ism, whatever that means; I took it as a compliment. Or the man who had obviously drank just enough to get the courage to open the door, but didn't come in much further, while declaring that Jesus is Lord, or the odd passersby who would walk just far enough to be at a safe distance while yelling back that we were going to hell. This may seem like a logical occurrence since Christians are taught to fear witchcraft, as an association with the devil. But this association also stems from a fear of bad magick. I have encountered at least a dozen instances where a self-proclaimed Christian tells me how they "used their mojo to make someone lose their job" or "prayed to God that he be punished" or "prayed that he would get what's coming to him". Simple enough, right? But what truly is being heard are forms of bad magick. Let me say that again, so that it really sinks in, you can practice bad magick without being a magickal practitioner.

I have only done bad magick once. I did it in the hopes of protecting a close friend of mine. The intention of my bad magick was virtuous, in my opinion, but that did not change the fact that it was bad magick. The day after casting my spell I strained my back at work. I leaned over in my chair, and felt as my lower back spasmed in pain. Because of this injury I left work early, and on the way home my car started making horrible noises. I drove

180

directly to the auto mechanic, which left me without transportation. Do you see where this is headed? Just wait there's more!

I decided to start walking towards my dad's house. When I got there I laid on the wood floor to rest my back, while petting my deaf cat Star. Star was a sweet soul, and would meow extremely loud since he had no sense of hearing. Star and I had forged a particularly strong bond because he was deaf, and I was able to talk to him psychically. Before I had started talking to him he was a bit skittish, but after, he became very loving and personable. He lay down next to me as I iced my back. Petting him and talking to my dad I started to feel better listening to him purr. The next thing I remember is a sharp stabbing feeling in my arm, and when I looked down Star had bitten me very deep and I was bleeding. I asked my dad to get me some hydrogen peroxide and a Band-Aid, but he had neither, so he brought me some toilet paper. I was beginning to feel embarrassed because it seemed so obvious that I had done bad magick, and I thought everyone would know.

The next day I went to work and during the course of the morning I realized that the red swelling around the puncture wound where Star bit me was getting worse. Some of my office mates told me it was infected, and that I needed to go to the doctor immediately. I left work, again. When I was at the doctor's office I received a tetanus shot and antibiotics. Over the next couple of days, the swelling went down, but I began to notice odd bruising on my legs and arms. I hadn't been bumping into anything, so I was concerned. I used a search engine to find the name of the antibiotic with the term 'unusual bruising'. The internet informed me I needed to visit my doctor immediately. Now at this point I could really only laugh as each new issue arose. I knew exactly why this was all happening! I knew as soon as I had seen the infection on my arm. It was bright red and in the shape of a heart around my tattoo, my 'healer's hand' tattoo! The heart that formed around that healer's hand was a blaring statement from the universe, "Use love, Healer! Not fear."

I told the universe that I knew I had done wrong, and I was willing to reap the consequences. The doctor told me I was having a reaction to this particular antibiotic and gave me a different one. Within the month I was no longer employed at my job, albeit I quit, but still there was so much that changed due to the spell I had cast. I knew I was never to try to fix someone else's problem in that way again. Let this be a lesson to you, it's not worth it! You can always find a way to solve the problem with love, always; you must use courage and insight to find the way that love is the answer, because it is.

Though I am opposed to using bad magick for any means, there is a grey (for lack of a better word) magick area that must be approached with caution. I find that I will often have to involve myself in grey magick as a means of protection. Possibly, in the future, I will be more evolved and know another, more efficient, way. This next story shows a little of what this grey magick looks like.

Back in my twenties I was a waitress and I met a wide variety of people. The most curious though, has to be the time I met a Satanist. This term may have multiple meanings to different people. In this story the Satanist was definitely someone who liked to participate in the Anton LaVey brand of Satanism. Whether or not you approve or disapprove of LaVeyan Satanism, for the purposes of this story know that this particular individual did not give me a good 'vibe'.

It was at the end of my swing shift, and I was getting side work done so that I could leave on time. A very handsome man walked in, mid-twenties, dark hair, six-foot, lean, and sat at the counter. As I brought him a coffee I noticed his upside-down pentacle, with goat head, necklace. Now, this is not necessarily a Satanist pendant, but in this particular situation I knew that it was. As I refilled the sugar dispenser by his seat he noticed the pentacle that I wore, and decided to strike up conversation, "Oh! You're a sister in the arts?! Nice to meet you."

"Yes, I do practice, but I'm not into what you're into," I reply, nodding over to his inverted pentagram.

"Now, now, there are many ways to play in the magickal sandbox," he retorts, with a charm that I knew had worked for him before.

"There might be many ways to play, but I'm not interested in yours." My response was definitive. I wasn't going to be swayed by someone who obviously used people for his own manipulations.

I heard his response in my head, rather than out loud, as he gave me a sly smile and sipped his coffee, "What a cute little witch." (Part of the reason I have such an aversion to Satanism, as well as other patriarchal systems of magick, is that there is an underlying belief that men are 'in charge' and that women, though cute, aren't as strong. This, in my opinion, is a continuation of the dominant paradigm within social norms. Witchcraft and Satanism lay outside of social norms, and so I would expect more differentiation, rather than applying a new face/name to the old system).

It was this remark that both flattered and pissed me off: his insinuation was that I wasn't as powerful as him, though he cloaked it in a whim of seduction. I put up my boundaries, finished my side work, and walked away from the diner that night realizing I had had a close call. I was sure I'd never see him again, and knew not to engage if I did. In his mind I was a 'little witch', something to play with, but that ultimately stood no match to his prowess; a cat batting a grasshopper. In fact, I was a little witch, I only had two years of practice under my belt. Intrinsically I knew I could beat him if I needed to, but preferred to keep that hypothesis untested.

The next day I was scheduled to work at the witchcraft store. I greeted the main witch of the store as I entered, and half-heartedly told her that I had met a stupid Satanist last night. As I told her the story, her eyes got big, and she asked, "Was his name Steven?"

"Yes," I said, sensing the tension rise in both myself, and the room.

"Was he tall, thin, dark hair?" she listed off all of his attributes. I nodded. She continued, "That guy is bad news! I'll have to let Sheila know he's back in town. He was stalking her that last time he was around. He must've gotten out of jail."

As the alarm began to ring in my head, I looked out the large window at the front of the store, and as if on cue there he was, Steven, walking towards our entrance. I dropped to the floor and crawled to the back room. Fuck! This guy was really fucking bad news, and now he was here. I felt the searing panic of an animal that was becoming prey, like electricity, up my spine. I listened as he entered the store, made small talk, asked about me, and was energetically directed out of the store. I was in trouble. He had marked me; I was his new play toy of interest. The main witch walked to the back and told me it was all clear, but in my mind I knew that it wasn't.

I knew the time to test my hypothesis had arrived. I have heard that necessity is the master of invention, and I believe it is also true that it is the creator of personal evolution. I remembered a not-quite-bad-magick spell I had learned from a friend of a friend. I knew this spell was only to be used in times of great need, and my intuition was yelling in my ear, "Now is that time!"

I told the main witch that I was going to take care of this, and went into the back with a black candle, a jar filled with water and my intention to cut any cords he had connected to me. I would disappear from his view, and he would go far, far, away from me.

I sat transfixed on the flame as I viewed him in my mind's eye, and as I did I kept hearing, "Such a cute little witch. Cute little witch." I heard it and became infuriated, my Italian blood boiled, and I began to psychically repeat a mantra of my own, "I am a cute little witch, and I'm going to defeat you. Look at this cute little witch cut all your power. Oh, what a cute little witch I am."

As my intensity grew, the main witch came back and looked at me, "What are you doing?"

"I'm getting rid of my problem." I spoke the words, without breaking my focus.

"Well shit, I can tell that, I just had no idea that guy actually practiced. I can smell the sulfur from here!" and with that she left me to finish my work.

The flame began to shift and jump, as if the Satanist thought he could escape, but he had already connected the cord between us, and I was using that connection to finish my task. As I continued my mantra the flame fought back, and I felt the engagement of magickal warfare tingle through my body. This man had decided to hunt the wrong little witch. The candle melted down, closer and closer to where the water would meet the flame, and our engagement intensified dramatically in those final seconds. I could hear him laughing in my head, and I was laughing back, with all my energetic stamina. As the water engulfed the flame, the struggle came to an end, and I laughed out loud (as per the instructions of the spell).

I walked to the front of the store with an air of accomplishment. The main witch looked at me astonished. I buried the jar of water with the extinguished candle across the street, and never saw the Satanist again. I heard, a few weeks later, that he had been run out of town by the cops.

This story is an example of how magickal protection can be necessary, especially if being threatened by another magickal practitioner, and feel in danger. This is a tenuous line though, as sometimes we will feel like someone is cursing or otherwise hurting us, when in actuality it is our own issues, or just life happening. Because of this tenuousness it is best to check yourself often, check in with yourself, and have others that you can rely on for honest feedback. I have heard many stories throughout history where a community will suspect witchcraft and go killing anyone that rises their suspicion. This is living in paranoia, and paranoia is not the desired outcome of a magickal lifestyle. If you find yourself living in paranoia it would be best to seek outside medical help.

Even retelling this story, I know that it was my best option at the time, but with greater healing and insight I may not use the same method again. When the danger is real, and the cord of a predator has connected to you, you must use your strongest means possible. The focus must not be in harming the other, but instead disconnecting, and protecting, yourself.

I hope, at this point in the chapter, that you can see bad magick is not a cut and dry topic. There are nuances, and contextual definitions that must be taken into account. A safe way to measure the degree of good or bad your spell resides in is to ask yourself, "What if someone was casting this against me?" I know, I know, that's the golden rule. I think it applies, though. I mean, no one really wants to think of magick being cast against them, but magick happens, all around, and you will be affected by it.

We cast magick with spells, and with thoughts. Anyone having a bad thought about you is effectively casting bad magick your way. Now, does this mean every angry thought you have is going to manifest? Not necessarily, but as you grow in your magickal abilities, your energy field will become stronger, and your strong thoughts will manifest. In my own practice I have come up with a technique to make sure I am not cursing every person who cuts me off; I know the feeling of intention-filled thought. I can feel when I am sending my thoughts out with intention, and I just cut off the energetic output, so that it does not manifest. We have angry thoughts, and when they arise, we look at them and find out what is the root of our anger.

Healing can be helped with a change in perspective. If you find yourself coming from a place of anger in your thoughts or interactions you must stop, take a breath, and realign yourself. Below is a kindness exercise, and is helpful when you feel you become taken up into the anger of the collective.

Kindness Exercise

Beauty and kindness are all around you and you will see it if you align yourself with the vibrations/energy of kindness. For this exercise I am having you begin to change your vibrations by changing your actions and tricking your mind. On a full moon you are to do a prayer ceremony where you birth beauty & kindness into your life.

1. Light a white tea-light candle, and take it outside when you can see the moon. Lift it high with your arms and call on the Goddess and the universe to bless it with beauty and kindness from all the cosmos.

2. Go back inside, and write down on a piece of paper one nice thing about each of the people you come into contact with on a daily basis, and then finish your list by writing one nice thing about yourself.

3. In a cauldron burn the piece of paper, and then burn some lavender on top of it

4. Over the next 3 days you are not allowed to say anything bad about

anyone, nor are you allowed to speak badly about yourself. This is a kindness exercise and it will bring kindness and beauty into your life, as well as make you very aware of the words you use on a daily basis, and what energy they carry. If you find yourself wanting to talk badly about others on a regular basis, then you are in practice of constantly bringing that baneful energy into your life. Change your actions, change your mind, and change your life.

15

Insights

As I live the magickal lifestyle I am constantly in awe of the unfolding mystery, and insights that present themselves. I do not have all the answers, but I know that if a question comes up, spirit will guide me to the knowledge I need. For me, magick is a profound interaction with all that is, and I can't imagine life any other way. At this point I hope that you realize that this book is less an instruction manual, and more a general guidance based on experience. You will have to make your own path; this is the gift of the magickal lifestyle.

The road is unique to each traveler, so mystical teachings tend to be obscure. Know that no one has all the answers. Sometimes when you are living the magickal lifestyle, and relying on your psychic senses, you won't even know that you're being psychic. Often you will find out later that a feeling you had was connected to a greater reality. For example, I was running a ceremony and I was trying to work the energy of the group into a cohesive whole. It was sort of a large group, and I was relatively new to running an open ceremony, so I was nervous, but focused. I was walking the interior while rattling, and keeping my head down so that I could feel more than see. I was focusing on creating an energetic mass that resonated together, and I was gathering it all in the center, to build this energy, before we sent it off. I walked the circle a couple of times, and felt this tug, this energetic dead zone every time I came to one spot. Feeling this, and knowing it was messing up the whole thing, I took a few steps back and really aggressively used my rattles to break up the energetic weakness. I kept my head down, rattling intensely while swaying, and as soon I felt the blockage release, I moved on. It was a successful ceremony, and I thought nothing more of it.

The next day one my students took me aside and asked me why I kept

In the Dark and the Light

TRUST WHAT YOU FEEL

doubt only

undermining intuition

The benefit of the

Your gut always knows, trust that knowledge.

Listen to your inner voice and learn how it speaks to you.

MEET YOURSELF

KNOW YOURSELF

Sacred Knowledge Increases When You believe

stopping in front of her friend in the circle. At first, I didn't know what she was talking about. She described the scenario again, and I realized that the lull in the energy was right where her friend was standing, a person she had brought to the open ritual. I told her that I was trying to get the energy moving, and it was stopping right in front of her friend. She was shocked and admitted, "I brought him because we're dating, but he doesn't believe in any of this stuff. He thought you were the devil."

I laughed uproariously; when I stopped in front of him during the ceremony, he had become afraid. I didn't know why I was stopping, all I knew was the feeling of a blockage, and it was my job to control the energy. My psychic senses didn't give me the whole story, probably because I would have been distracted by such animosity. To him, though, I knew everything. The theme of this story happens to me the most: I feel something, and react to feelings, but the people around me think I know *everything*. Don't fall for this assumption. Trust your own senses above all else, and know that the whole story may never present itself.

Interacting with magick will make you more sensitive. You are co-creating your reality, and awareness of this truth gives you tools to be able to affect change. There are always multiple possibilities brewing at any one time, and if you learn to be sensitive to their vibrations, you can put your energy into the possibility that you prefer, and lay the foundation for a new world. Always try to lead with your heart, so that your energy stays light, and vibrant.

You must pursue the spirit in life, or you will become stagnant in the vibration of your own self-absorption. Spirit reaches out, and you must listen; listen in order to pursue, and engage. One of the greatest accomplishments a human can have in this incarnation is to pay attention, truly. Have you been paying attention? Magick is happening all around you. Pursuing your goals is worthwhile, but will strike a flat cord unless you also keep yourself open to the mysteries of the universe changing your life. You will never be able to control everything, and that should not be your goal.

All of magick is experienced in that ineffable moment that you allow your body, mind and soul to commune with the world of energy. To surrender to that moment is to become one with all that is. Of course I don't expect you to become enlightened, but moments of enlightenment are embodied in this surrender.

In that moment you know truth, you know the truth of lies, and you know exactly what to do; there is no questioning, only interacting. Once you are interacting with spirit you realize that you are regularly in acquaintance with magick! It is all around you and happening at every moment, accepting it as a world of energy, and your place within it puts you in community, and in touch with power. You will no longer fall prey to lies, deceit, and ulterior motives. To know yourself, and the world around you, is to be aware of its complete beauty and simplicity. Knowing this truth allows you to realize when others are perpetuating the traumas of their youth; manipulation, lies, and preying on weakness. It is not because they are bad people, necessarily, but because they have grown up learning a system that is broken and relies on manipulation and deceit to survive. You must have compassion in your revelations about the truths of yourself and others, and at the same time realize that you are no longer allowed to be an enabler in someone else's self-deceit.

The techniques detailed in this book are designed to bring you closer to the spirit, and interaction with the divine, the world of living energy, but you must ultimately surrender, you must push past the fear and journey forward, always, or always be striving. To enact true magick, and amazing feats of life change, you must surrender. Let yourself fall into the great abyss of energy. Know that you will always have a spark of creation within you, and that spark is you, it is what you created your personality and ego from; and it will always remain true to itself so let go, let go, fall in, raise your arms to the heavens fall to your knees, let yourself make love to the spirit; open, receive, surrender.

In the surrender you embrace the power of your own life: paradox. Always embrace the paradoxes, and once you can bring your brain to accept both segments of the truth, then you are one with the universe. Become a bridge, between ideas, and between worlds.

Becoming a bridge person means that you will need to start bridging aspects within yourself. You must realize power within silence. It is the only way to know yourself completely. When you can silence the chatter of your mind, the constant desire to self-define through thoughts, you will know who you are at your core. I still find myself struggling with this concept. I too will fall back into old patterns of insecurity, and then my mind will take them and run. To live a magickal lifestyle is to know when your thoughts are getting the best of you, and to realize that they will not always be that way. You must take back the power within yourself, and search out your life's purpose.

All of the world is made up of mundane objects on top of sacred frequencies. All of the world is sacred, and the mundane rests on top of it, in all things. Shifting consciousness will allow you to perceive it, and in the perception there is reverence. Walking between the worlds is being able to shift your consciousness at will. After a while you will also be able to shift your paradigm at will.

Though the sacred is everywhere, there are also places of power. These places resonate with magick stronger than most. You travel to places of power for specific sacred purposes; Ley lines, vortexes, power centers. These places carry more of the mystery, more energetic resonance, and are utilized for magickal purposes. Do not engage with a power center if you are not ready for the responsibility, and consequences of your action. I don't say that to make you afraid, but you must be aware that magick will change your life. Engaging the mystery requires you to let go of control, and know that you will be taken on a wild adventure.

With that being said, it is also true that to engage on a journey with the mysteries, one must disengage their desire to predict each moment. In mundane life each moment follows the next linearly, and you can predict times' continuance. In the world of magick you must be open and aware when time feels different, and when life propels you in a new direction. I find I am often being required to take a leap of faith, and with each leap I become more understanding of how magick works, and the beauty of trusting implicitly everything in the universe. To trust is not to allow things to abuse you, you do not trust by allowing lies, you trust yourself to know the truth of all things, and it is that trust that you put in the universe, and yourself, with each leap of faith.

Magick is a decision that you must decide to engage in. No one is forced into this life, however, if you have great sensitivity and you give in to fear, and opt for a mundane life, you will also abandon the gifts of the universe that are part of your birthright. Why am I telling you all of this? Because you need to understand why magick doesn't work

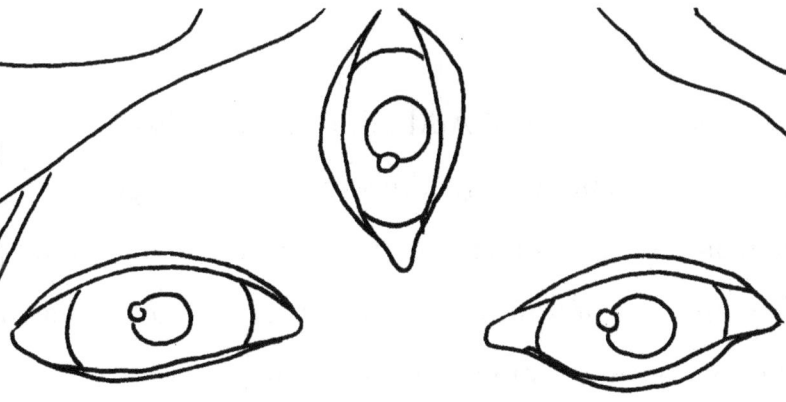

Choose the moral of your story and Adhere to its Virtues & Values

KNOW YOURSELF

PERSPECTIVE

Know that there are systems of oppression in society— they are real and they are harmful and at the same time do not let your story be directed by giving over your power

VICTIM

Do not judge those who are victims to their story, but don't become a victim.

If you do not agree with the moral of the story then rewrite the story.

Your story can always be changed by shifting your perspective. You can always be empowered with recipes alone. Recipes are fun! Add oil, and herbs to an object, dress it up and hope it works. The crucial ingredient to every magick recipe is giving yourself over to it; it is part of you that is working magick and as such it must be within you, vibrating out of you, into the universe. You must also forget the magick after you've done it. View the experience of complete surrender as the gift of magick workings. Allow your body to feel the joy and passion of release. Train your mind that you are always in communion with the divine, and you will let go of controlling the outcome. These are the mysteries of life and magick. This is why not everyone does it, tremendous courage is needed to surrender to your true form. Some do it naturally, but for most of us we have to make a conscientious decision to fall into the great unknown, to give up the reins.

To engage in the magickal lifestyle you must be willing to interact with the spirits, and heed their messages. If you don't like something they say, then you can decide against it, and tell them why. You are allowed to be an agent of your own will. If you have a good reason not to act, then that is respectable, and in some cases was a test to see if you would just follow all directions blindly. Never! Know yourself, and your morals, know how far you will go and why. The spirits respect your knowledge. Many times they view the world differently, and so see nothing wrong with a particular action, but it may be the wrong action for you. Further, sometimes you're just not ready to take the next step in a journey towards personal evolution, and that's fine too. It is better to learn, and decide, then to go unwittingly, and lose your will.

Physical action and silence are two very important aspects of the magical lifestyle that sometimes get forgotten. Physical action is absolutely imperative in order to move the energy in your body. If you are doing magick, then you are embodying a large amount of energy, and that energy will stagnate into sickness if you don't keep it moving. I enjoy doing yoga to release any build-ups, and keep my energy body flowing. Find a physical activity that works for you, and make the practice a magickal ritual in and of itself.

Silence is necessary to get you back in touch with your inner core. It is very tempting to become addicted to stimulus: media, songs, chatting with friends. With technological advancements growing rapidly you must make a concerted effort to find silence, preferably near nature. I like to take little adventures to the nearby mountain, often to gather magickal ingredients, but mostly to reconnect with my own silence.

If you can combine your physical action with silence you will find inside of you is a well of information waiting to burst forth. Every worry, every thought that you've had, invokes answers, and in the silence of your bodily movement they all float to the surface, to be acknowledged and released. You will feel lighter, and more vibrant when you allow yourself these two activities. They are necessary for your health and survival, *especially* if you work with magick. Having greater access to large amounts of energy requires greater responsibility, and actions to keep yourself in balance.

Now that we are at the end of this book, know that the magick's been inside of you all along! There is a whole world of love and support in the ethereal and they are excited to work with you. Go forth on this journey knowing that many have come before you, and many will come after you. You are an ancestor of the future, and the ancestors of the past will guide you into your destiny.

Glossary

Altar: An altar is a space that has been designated as sacred, and arranged to make magick. In the Peruvian tradition, an altar is a mesa, a sacred bundle that carries power objects, and represents the world of the carrier. There are different specific uses of the mesa, depending on how it is arranged. I find myself making altars of all the flat spaces in my home. I will clear some space, and build an altar with significant items that represent the working that I want to do. I often have more than one altar going, at a time.

Altered Consciousness: To alter your consciousness means to step out of normal reality, or to perceive reality differently than usual. Your consciousness has generally been trained to a consensual reality, one where the ether is a different realm. When you enter into altered consciousness, you realize that the ether is the unseen world that exists in tandem with the physical realm; the ether like an invisible blanket that exists on top of normative reality.

Archetype: Archetypes are symbols that show up over and over in the stories of life. Each archetype is made up of a core set of characteristics, and has a life-lesson associated with it. The hero, the trickster, the fool, and the warrior are some examples. Often times, in the magickal lifestyle, one may find themselves often playing an archetypical role in their interactions. To fully embrace, and find the power in, the archetype, one must first acknowledge it, and then ask themselves why they like to play that role.

Bridge Person: A bridge person is someone that walks between the worlds, is a bridge between the mundane, and the ethereal. Often times a shaman is called one who walks with one foot in each world, and in Wicca, when creating sacred space to practice magick, it is said to be between the worlds. A bridge person is a connector, that helps heal people, and show them what they cannot see. A bridge between the right and left brains, the head and the heart, the root and the crown.

Cleansing: In the magickal lifestyle, one must be always concerned with their cleansing, releasing unwanted energies from their energetic field. In order to do a cleansing, one must find a technique that works for them. I find the easiest to be a salt bath, but there are many, many more ways to do it. As one gains energy, and power, in the magickal lifestyle, they become more sensitive to energetic vibrations, and cleansing becomes a necessary routine.

Cosmology: A cosmology refers to the belief in how the universe, and cosmos works. Modern cosmology relies on science, and science is dictated by western thought. In this way, even though science practices the scientific method as a means of staving off subjectivity, science is still not completely unbiased. I like to refer to the term cosmology as how one believes the world, and the cosmos, work. Religion hasn't always been differentiated from science, and many cosmologies have a religious basis. So, though it is a bit of a scientifically blasphemous usage, I use cosmology as in religious understanding of how the universe works. For example, Buddhists believe that the Earth is balanced on the back of a turtle, and as such, I think that qualifies as a cosmology.

Deviance: Deviance is simply a break from social norms. When someone doesn't act like society expects them to, they are being deviant. Because the practice of the magickal lifestyle is not a social norm (currently), to engage in it is to engage in deviance. I would like to point out, however, that mystical traditions exist in every single dominant religious paradigm, and the mystical experience is very similar to the magickal lifestyle. Mystical traditions, though, tend to not be the normative practice, if even acknowledged by the dominant religion that they belong to.

Energetic Field: Your energetic field is the energy that you carry with you, and that surrounds you. Some call it an aura, or a soul, but I prefer energy field because I find that fully encompasses what I am referring to. When someone's energetic resonance is affecting you, then it is in your field. When you are thinking about something, that thing is now in your field. I believe there are books written on the aura, and it has more than one layer, and nuanced meaning.

Ether: Ether, as in the ethereal, is the unseen world that exists on top of normative reality. The ether can be in dreamtime, or on planes of existence that don't seem to be earthlike. Many have pointed to the ethers as being the heavens, however, in my understanding the micro reflects the macro, all of heaven exists right now, right here.

Gender Norms: Gender norms are society's expectations of the behavior or men and women. Human characteristics, such as courage, nurture, leader, weak, are assigned to the categories of masculine and feminine. It is expected that men are masculine, and women are feminine. These gendered expectations become internalized into the people being socialized into society, so that they will decide whether they are allowed to act one way, or another. Gender norms are supposed to help society function smoothly, and are often considered biologically determined, however, gender norms are different depending on which society you are looking at. Because gender norms are not the same in every human society across the globe, and throughout time, then we can see that they are actually socially constructed.

Magick: I spell magick with a 'k' because during my graduate studies, the chair of my thesis committee asked me if my work was on magic tricks, or sleight of hand. Ever since that experience, I have felt it is very important to differentiate magic from magick, as magick is a real experience, and *not* an illusion. Magick is to create change on the physical realm by putting out energized intention on the ethereal realm. When *The Secret* (2006) spoke of your thoughts dictating your reality, the basic premise is that everything is magick. When a magickal practitioner does magick, there is specific intention and effort put forth to create a manifestation.

Moon Cycle: The moon cycle is very obvious is you've ever watched the moon. It changes daily as it waxes (gets bigger), and wanes (gets smaller). In society, most people will know when it is a full moon, that auspicious time that is shrouded in mystery. The moon cycles are all important though, and they denote the energies that are useful for magick. The full moon is to give birth, or to manifest. The waning moon is release. The waxing moon is to grow. The dark moon is working in the dark, and whatever that means to you. The darkness can also be one's subconscious, and so dark moon magick can focus on healing hidden issues. The new moon is used for new beginnings, and planting seeds.

Mysteries: The mysteries are aspects of life that can't be understood through the mind, only comprehended through the experience. The mysteries encapsulate everything that governs life, the lessons that are often in plain sight, but taken for granted, or not seen clearly. The mysteries is the ineffable, that which cannot be spoken, but must be understood to progress in magick.

Normative Reality: Normative reality is the expected experience that society agrees upon. Society generally doesn't believe that a human can speak to animals, or that psychic awareness is real. To engage in the magickal lifestyle, you have to disengage with normative reality.

Raising Energy: In order to practice magick, you must raise energy towards your goal. Similarly, a prayer is more powerful is there is more feeling to it. Raising energy is a concerted effort to bring up the vibration in a magickal working, so that it can be released towards the end goal. I have found that raising energy is difficult if everyone involved isn't totally into it. Knowing whether or not energy is being raised relies on your self-awareness: can you feel the energy flow? Is it strong, or stuck? Where is it stuck, and can you push past the blockage? Often a blockage of energy flow will occur if you are actually afraid of the magick coming true.

Social Norms: Society's expectations of behavior. Generally social norms are created to keep society running smoothly; everyone knows the expected way to interact, and so we know what is expected, and the underlying meaning. Social norms, however, sometimes reproduce inequality, or perpetuate an un-empowered aspect of reality. By deviating from social norms, one is able to question the social system, and get others to question it as well.

Spells: A spell is the act of engaging in magick. I have been doing research into the difference between spells, and prayers, and have found the only difference to be social expectation. A spell is bad, because it is magick, and a prayer is good because it is part of the social norm. Researching the different reasons that people pray (Baesler, 2002) I found that they were really no different than why people do magick. The only difference seemed to be who was being prayed to.

Web of Energy: All of life is connected through the web of energy, where everything has an energy field, and each interaction, connection pulses in communication with each other. Each mystical tradition has a different name for it, but basically everything is comprised of energy, and energy lines shoot out of energetic beings with intention.

Suggested Reading

As I mention throughout this book, there are many other books that are wonderful for expanding your knowledge on the ways of magick. Below is a list of books that I have found helpful, and informative.

1. The Ayahuasca Experience: A Sourcebook on the Sacred Vine of Spirits, edited by Ralph Metzner (1999)
2. The Red of His Shadow, by Mayra Montero (2001)
3. Vodou in Haitian Life and Culture: Invisible Powers, Edited by Claudine Michel and Patrick Bellegarde-Smith (2006)
4. Italian Witchcraft: The Old Religion of Southern Europe by Raven Grimassi
5. Masters of Living Energy: The Mystical World of the Q'ero of Peru, by Joan Parisi Wilcox (1999)
6. The Path of the Energetic Mystic: Part 1 A Key to Open Your Heart, by Inge Teunissen, and Dennis Alejo Mango (2013)
7. Tales from the Night Rainbow, by Koko Willis and Pali Jae Lee (2001)
8. Siddhartha, by Hermann Hesse (1951)
9. The Witch's Dream, by Florinda Donner-Grau (1997)
10. The Power of Myth, by Joseph Campbell (1991)
11. The Witch of Portobello, by Paulo Coelho (2007)
12. The Andean Codex: Adventures and Initiations among the Peruvian Shamans, by J.E. Williams (2005)
13. Book of Shadows, by Phyllis Curott (1998)
14. The Alchemist, by Paulo Coelho (1993)
15. Encyclopedia of Magical Herbs, by Scott Cunningham (1990)

References

Adler, Margot. (1996) *Drawing Down the Moon Witches, Druids, Goddess-Worshippers, and Other Pagans in America.* New York, NY: Penguin Books.

Baesler, James E. (2002) Prayer and Relationship with God II: Replication and Extension of the Relational Prayer Model. *Review of Religious Research,* 44 (1), 58-67.

Buckland, Raymond. (2002) *Buckland's Complete Book of Witchcraft.* St. Paul, MN: Llewellyn Publications.

Byrne, Rhonda. (2006) *The Secret.* New York, NY: Atria Books.

Castaneda, Carlos. (1968) *The Teachings of Don Juan: A Yaqui Way of Knowledge.* New York, NY: Washington Square Press.

_____. (1971) *A Separate Reality.* New York, NY: Washington Square Press.

_____. (1994, March) You Only Live Twice. *Details Magazine.* Found at http://www.nagualism.com/you-only-live-twice.html

Coelho, Paulo. (1993) *The Alchemist.* Hammersmith, London: HarperCollins

Coelho, Paulo. (2008) *The Witch of Portobello: A Novel.* Hammersmith, London: HarperCollins

Cunningham, Scott. (2002) *Earth, Air, Fire, and Water: More Techniques of Natural Magic.* St. Paul, MN: Llewellyn Publications

_____. (1990) *Encyclopedia of Magical Herbs.* St. Paul, MN: Llewellyn Publications.

_____. (2004) *Wicca: A Guide for the Solitary Practitioner.* St. Paul, MN: Llewellyn Publications.

Curott, Phyllis. (1998) *Book of Shadows: A Modern Woman's Journey into the Wisdom of Witchcraft and the Magic of the Goddess.* New York, NY: Broadway Books.

Grimassi, Raven. (2000) *Encyclopedia of Wicca and Witchcraft.* St. Paul, MN: Llewellyn Publications.

_____. (1999) *Hereditary Witchcraft: Secrets of the Old Religion.* St. Paul, MN: Llewellyn Publications.

_____. (2003) *Italian Witchcraft: The Old Religion of Southern Europe.* St. Paul, MN: Llewellyn Publications.

Greenwood & Airey (2006) *The Complete Illustrated Encyclopedia of Witchcraft & Practical Magic.* London, UK: Hermes House.

Harner, Michael J. (1980). *The Way of the Shaman: A Guide to Power and Healing.* San Francisco, CA: Harper & Row.

Johnstone, Ronald L. (2007) *Religion in Society: A Sociology of Religion.* New York, NY: Routledge.

Mitchell, Stephen. (1992). *Tao Te Ching.* New York, NY: HarperCollins.

www.ingramcontent.com/pod-product-compliance
Lightning Source LLC
Chambersburg PA
CBHW062111090426
42741CB00016B/3387